The
Story and Poems
of the Boy from
DINGLE
HOLE ROAD

The
Story and Poems
of the Boy from
DINGLE
HOLE ROAD

Al Luckette

YorkshirePublishing
www.yorkshirepublishing.com
Write Now.

ISBN: 978-1-947247-56-7
The Story and Poems of the Boy from Dingle Hole Road
Copyright © 2017 by Al Luckette.

Yorkshire Publishing
3207 South Norwood Avenue
Tulsa, Oklahoma 74135
www.YorkshirePublishing.com
918.394.2665

For
My wife *Fran*
and kids *Carolyn*, *Angela*, and *Michael*

Table of Contents

11   *Introduction*

13   The Early Years

23   Dingle Hole Road

37   Country Schooling

56   The Trailer Trip West

75   Back to Syracuse

79   Manlius Center Store

85   Boy Scouts

89   The Dog Pound

95   Garage Worker

97   Restaurant Business

107   Raising Chickens

113   How I Met the KKK

117   Out of Florida

123   Restarting in New York

137   Evangelistic Understudy

149   One More Trip

159   Conclusion of the Matter

163   I am One of Those

165   My Song is Jesus

167   Sunday Morning

169   The Preaching of the Word

171   Jesus Will see You Through

173   Prepare Yourself

175   Jesus is the Only Way

177   What Does it Profit?

179   Lord, Carry Me

181   Where Your Treasure Is

185   A Million Years from Now

186   Forgive

189   Voice in the Wilderness

191   My Storm

193   Are we growing?

195   Back home

197   Baptize me

201   Busy

203   Called out

205   Church people

207   Do you believe Jesus

209   Double mindedness

211   Foolish little thoughts

213   Gossip

215   He rescued me

217   He wrote my name in the sand

219   Heavenly trip.

221   I've got Resurrection living in my soul

223   I must be somebody special

225   I will never leave Thee.

227   Is your heart set on things Heavenly?

229   Jack

233   Just Another Day

235   Life

237   No one can pluck me out of his hand

239   Noah and the Ark

241   Noah

243   Peter And The Master

245   Sleepy world

247   The friend I never had

249   The hand of God

251   The Moon into Blood

253   The wicked heart

257   The worried heart.

259   The yard sale

261   A Man I knew

263   Today I shall be Happy

265   Who is that stranger?

271   Wise man.

273   You can't fool God.

275   My mom

279   Hard times.

281   Dingle Hole Road

Introduction

WHEN I CALL SOMEONE ON THE PHONE, I ANNOUNCE myself as Al Luckette from Kirkville, New York. Almost nobody really understands why I use this introduction. I get a few laughs about it, and some even mimic me by giving me their address with their full name. There was a time in my life, though, when I wasn't sure where I would be tomorrow. A time between, oh let's say age four to my teen years. My father was the catalyst throughout this era, and this book is not about him, but me. He is the driving force in the book, the one that propelled my family from place to place. He tried every thing you could imagine, and some things you couldn't. He owned and operated restaurants, he had garages, he had stores, he operated a private detective agency, and studied law. He even had an evangelistic ministry. When he was in his late twenties, he built homes in the Carolinas. Later he remodeled in the French quarters in New Orleans. Sometimes, now, I think of my life as a boy on a rollercoaster. I was on a wild ride that seemed to have no end, hanging on to the bar on the front of the coaster car, being lifted then dropped; everyone around watching the ride, some shaking their heads, some holding their mouths gasping at the wild turns and loops.

During this time of my life I never had anyone outside the family as a friend, although I met some interesting people and had temporary friends for very short periods of time. I am the oldest of ten children born to my parents. All my siblings experienced some of the same things I did but not to the same degree. They would tell you they were on the rollercoaster, but they had back seats. I sat up front.

After my marriage at age twenty, both my wife and I got saved. And eventually I became a minister of the Gospel, now for over thirty years. We have three children, two girls and a boy, and three grandsons. I worked in a factory to supplement my income and retired with a small pension. We live in the suburbs of Syracuse, New York, in a community called Kirkville. But I didn't always live in Kirkville, and that's my story.

I named the book Dingle Hole Road for a couple reasons. One, I lived on Dingle Hole road during my early years and probably spent more time there than any other place before my sixteenth birthday. I grew up on Dingle Hole Road, and it prepared me for my ride through my early years. Secondly, the name "Dingle Hole Road" seems to denote something like a hole in the wall place, out of the way, or out of place. It surely was located at the end of the world; it could have been called Timbuktu or Shangri-La. It's all the same. In it's time it was the lowest point on earth for me, and the highest point of my early life after I left it. I learned responsibility and how to work with my hands. I was six when we moved there and almost nine when we left. I had always felt the hand of God in my life, how he protected me, and watched me. Several times I faced death and God pulled me through. He knows the future, and man can not undo what he has a design on. Now, let's see, where should we start? How about at the beginning?

The early years

Early in the morning of May 22, 1944, I was born on the fifth floor in Memorial hospital, in Syracuse, New York. We didn't live in Syracuse very long after that. Our family moved to the south, where my dad had a business somewhere in the Carolinas building homes. We jumped around a little before I was two, but at one point, dad was shot in the leg with a forty-five pistol. That brought us back to Syracuse. We lived with my dad's mother in town; she was a wonderful person with a deep, full faith. Grandma spoke with broken English. She was firm and wasn't afraid to speak her mind. Her weakness was her family. She tried to help out even when the problems were overwhelming. My father had his leg in a cast. We lived there; mom, dad, and at this point three kids (my sister Regina, my brother Paul, and myself) in a small upstairs apartment. To add to the dilemma, my aunt moved in with a bunch of kids because of a spat with her husband. I still remember that small apartment, even though I was not much over three years old. We slept on the floor, on blankets, and played with our cousins in the dining room.

My uncles would visit, Uncle Louie, and his brother John. Uncle John Luckette had just recently gotten out of the army and would come around wearing his uniform. He was a medic who served under General Patton. Uncle Louie was a prizefighter, and every session was boxing lessons. I learned to jab and hook before I was four. My uncles liked to tease me about a boogieman. They would tease me asking what I would do if I met the boogieman. Then I would tell them how I would defend myself by throwing left jabs at the air, saying I would do this or that. Then Uncle John would come to the door knocking. My dad and Uncle Louie would say, "It's the boogieman! Run!"

Panic overcame me I would scream and attempt to hide somewhere in the apartment. When the door opened, Uncle John had his hat pulled down over his face and in a low growl would call my name. They would put me in a guitar case and close the top. It was a horrifying experience, but I mention it because it is so vivid in my memory, and I carried the fear of close places for a long time.

This went on for a while, and then we moved. This time we ended up in New Orleans. Dad was involved in the construction business again. He had an office with a big fan, and that's all I knew about his job. My sister Linda was born while we lived there. We had a small, one room apartment; there was a bed on one side, a couch in the middle, and a kitchenette on the other side. A wire was strung over the middle of the room with a green army blanket hanging as a divider. My mother had a midwife come when she delivered Linda. Like it happened yesterday, Regina, Paul, and I sat on the couch just feet from the blanket. We heard our mother moan and groan, then the baby screaming. The midwife said it was a girl! We looked at each other, in amazement, now there was four.

Christmas Car Fire

For some reason we had to make a hasty retreat out of town. It was winter, our car was loaded, we sat on piles of clothes and tools and junk. Back then there were no super highways; you traveled on state roads, which passed through the towns. Our route took us to Hagerstown, Maryland. It was Christmas Eve and snowing hard, the weather was very cold when we approached a traffic light on the top of the hill in the heart of the town. As we attempted to go, the car exploded and burst into flames. We scrambled from the car, my mom carrying Linda and dragging little Paulie. Regina and I were pulled from the car by my father. We were poorly dressed for the weather and were shivering in the blowing snow. Almost instantly there were fire trucks and Policemen everywhere. Regina and I had been looking at all the Christmas lights just before the fire, and it took a few moments to come to realize that it was Christmas. The police took us to the station for a warm glass of chocolate milk. Then one of the policemen called a fireman over to us and asked if he could take some of us home for the night.

I ended up going to his house for the night. The fireman had a son my age. They had a beautiful ranch-styled home, neatly decorated for the season. There was a Christmas tree with an electric train around the base on the floor. The son wanted to show me his train, but I was hungry, tired, and confused by the night's happenings. The fireman's wife directed the boy to take me into his room to get me some clothes. I followed him into a clean, small room with a bed, dresser, and a closet. He took from the dresser a pair of socks and pants and a shirt. It was his own room; I was amazed and wondered at having one's own dresser in his own room. It was beyond my comprehension. I had up to now only had things in a shopping bag. The only socks I had were the ones I wore.

Everything we owned was destroyed in the fire. The town gave us the money to get back to Syracuse. It was a train ride out of town. The only thing I really remember about the ride was Paul and I running up and down the isle of the train car. So, back to Syracuse we went. We lived right on the end of Park Avenue on West Street. From our house it was a straight walk to the first school I attended. Frasier School was located on the other end of Park Ave., about eight blocks from our house. I had learned to write my name before I went into school. I guess being the oldest, my mother spent more time with me, teaching me my letters and numbers. I liked to draw, even then, and would draw cars and houses and would spend hours alone in a corner just drawing.

We stood in the snow and watched our car burn to the ground on Christmas eve.

Starting School

The first day of school was a rude awakening for me. My parents spent a lot of energy telling me what to expect; my mother even taught me to tie my shoes before I started school. She would say, "You can't go to school if you can't tie your shoes." When I learned, she would make me show off my shoe-tying talent to anyone and everyone, then highlighted the event with the remark, "Now he's ready for school." If I had an idea what I was getting into, I would have resisted the lessons. Mom and I walked down Park Ave. to the school. We met the teacher, we had the tour of the room, and then my mother gave me a hug and a kiss and started out. I was not ready for this; I made a scene (that's putting it mildly.) So for the first week she stayed all day. That weekend she rehearsed how I would be all right alone and could play with the blocks and draw on the chalkboard. Everything was good up to the moment she tried to sneak out. I saw her out on the sidewalk, and I went berserk. I bolted to the door; she heard my screaming and returned. She had to stay with me up to October 31st. That day I told her I could do it alone. I never thought about the other kids at home; they had to have someone watching them for almost two months. One day after my mother left me in the school, I planned an escape. I reached the main doorway ahead of the teacher. In those days the doors swung in, and I couldn't open the door. She swooped me up and carried me back under her arm. I was kicking and screaming; I was terrified of staying there.

One day the teacher had us sitting in a circled group. She was reading a story from a book when one of the girls in front of me peed her pants. The stream began to move my way. The teacher could not see the problem but was watching me very closely because of my past attempted escapes. I became very excited. I knew she would holler at me if I so much as moved a muscle, but if I stayed sitting there I would surely be carried away in the coming river. Suddenly, I bolted to the door screaming at the top of my lungs. She was right behind me. I guess I've been afraid of women ever since. She learned about the pee when we returned to the room and apologized to me. I remember her telling the other teachers what happened, and they all got a good laugh over it. They all treated me pretty good after that. Sometimes my mother would give me a dime to take the bus; it was a nickel each way.

My dad had a garage at 110 Wellington place in Syracuse. He was doing mechanic and body work. He had a young man working for him named Ken Cox. Ken was about eighteen and could not read or write. One morning Ken was having coffee with us as I was getting ready for kindergarten. Dad was bragging about how I could spell certain words, "spell salt," he ordered, and I would spell, "s-a-l-t" slowly. "Spell spoon," he said, pointing to a spoon on the table. "S-p-o-o-n," I spelled back. Then he turned to Ken and said, "Spell milk, Ken." Ken looked around the table; there was a bottle of milk, you know the old type with the bubble on the top that held the cream, and a can also of evaporated milk. My father always used evaporated milk in his coffee. Ken looked at the bottle then the can, then the bottle. He turned to my father and with a puzzled look asked, "What kind of milk do you want me to spell?" I never forgot that, and later when someone asked for milk for their coffee, we would ask what kind of milk they wanted.

We moved to Baldwinsville before kindergarten ended, so I finished Kindergarten there. The school was called Elizabeth Street School. On my sixth birthday, my parents had a party. It was one of the only parties I ever had. It was a big party; there seemed to be a hundred people there. The only gift I remember was a fishing pole. One of my father's friends was a junk collector he had a huge truck. He parked the truck right in front of the house. I was outside playing with some friends, when my mother called me in. The house was full of people, and they were all shouting happy birthday to me. I was so surprised, and there were gifts setting on the coffee table in the front room. One by one I opened the gifts. There were cards with money, there were little cars and trucks, and different writing and drawing materials. Everyone wanted me to open their gift and then explain how I would like it. Then there was this one gift in a long package, I opened it and there it was, a red fishing pole, with a reel and fishing hook. There were a lot of neighborhood kids there and they were as excited about the gifts as I was, but when I opened the fishing pole gift, one of the kids could not contain himself any longer. He grabbed the pole and shot out the door. I gave chase, and the boy ran behind the big truck and tossed my fishing pole in the back of the truck. He ran across the street to his home. I turned from the chase to retrieve my pole. I climbed onto the back bumper and tried to lift myself onto the bed of the truck. I was tired from chasing the boy and didn't realize how high the back bed was. I was going to get that pole back one way or the other, but on the corner of the back gate there was a jagged piece of steel sticking up on the deck of the truck bed. I looked into the back of the truck and saw my fishing pole up towards the middle of the truck. Then suddenly I felt a sharp pain in my right arm just above my elbow. I looked at my arm and it was bleeding something terrible. I panicked and jumped from the truck. I hit the ground with a thud, then picked myself up and ran screaming to the house. I ran into the front room where the crowd was and was crying hysterically. My mother grabbed me and began screaming herself. "What happened!, What happened!," she screamed. "I cut myself on the truck" I cried. Some of the guests stood and looked at the truck through the front room window. They said I must have cut myself in the back of the truck, as I ran past it, because it looked pretty jagged. My mother took me into the kitchen and began to wash the cut. She was saying, "I don't know, I don't know." My father came in and helped wrap the cut. I cried through the whole thing, and was so tired I laid on my bed and sniffled myself to sleep. I could hear the guests in the other room all talking about my ordeal. When someone new came in they would be told, "you missed all the action." I must have slept for about an hour. When I awoke and reappeared into the front room, those who were still there greeted me with smiles and asked how I felt. I told them I was feeling better and would like some cake and ice cream. I didn't think about it right away, but the junk dealer had left, and with him my red fishing pole. For some time the scar on my arm was a long red mark from my elbow half way to my shoulder. It looked like my little red fishing pole. I carry that scar to this day, I call it my birthday wound.

We seemed to have a lot of friends in the neighborhood in Baldwinsville. At night some people would come over and my father would get out his guitar and sing songs. My father was a pretty good singer and attracted the women, and my mother didn't like that. He sang a song about a goat that ate shirts from a clothesline and then coughed them up and flagged down a train. Dad would cut our hair with clippers just like a barber and sometimes cut hair for the boys in the neighborhood. There was one family with a bunch of boys, most of them were older than me, but we played baseball and kickball in the street. My brother Paul was hit with a bat when he walked into the home baseline. He got an awful scar on his forehead, but he was all right. It was at that time they started to have ice cream trucks come around the neighborhood. Sometimes there would be about thirty kids on one corner, all waiting for an ice cream. In that hot summer of my life, I remember the ice cream truck, but we never had any money to actually buy any ice cream from the driver, but it was games and fun, and Regina and I would run out to the truck just to see the other kids. I think there were others there that couldn't afford to buy anything, but the music from the truck seemed to initiate a call for game time. One of the popular games we played was kick the can. Even as a kindergartener, I was allowed to play with the older kids. I passed into first grade and remember how proud I was to bring home the paper saying I would be going into first grade.

Dingle Hole Road

Near the end of that summer we moved out of Baldwinsville, to Phoenix, New York. The house was located just outside of town on Dingle Hole Road. The family with the boys helped us move in a large, old truck, with all our possessions, on a hot day. Some of the boys rode in the back of the truck on the piles of clothes. When we got there it took only a short time to unload. Ma had things piled into the very small house, two small bedrooms, and a kitchen. The house had no electricity or running water. We weren't there a half-hour when my father assembled a kite and had it up; it was windy. The kite kept twirling, and my father kept adding more tail. He was totally engulfed in flying that kite. Meantime, mom and I were looking over the situation we were in. When we began to look around in the house, we noticed there were no wall switches for the lights. The kitchen sink had no faucets. There was a single lantern on the counter next to the sink. Ma kind of laughed and said something about not having to worry about the utility bills being too high. There was more, no toilet in the house. There was a small shed in the back about twenty yards from the house; I was informed that it was the toilet. I still remember the smell when I first opened the door! Unbelievable! It was a small room about four feet by three feet. A board about two feet high ran along the back; it had two round holes that would be the family toilet for over three years, summer and winter. The front yard had a well; it was covered with a four by eight sheet of plywood. To extract water you threw a pail with a rope attached down the hole, after sliding the plywood aside, then pulled the pail up with the water. All the time we lived there, we had to fetch the water from the well. Winters were tough, because you had to get close to the well hole and not slip in because of the ice. Sometimes there was so much snow we couldn't get water till we got the well cover shoveled off. I was six when we moved there, and I learned to get the water right off. My mother was terrified that I went near the hole, but my Dad thought it was okay, and someone had to do it anyway. Dingle Hole Road was the beginning of my age of responsibility. Before I was seven I would take on responsibilities that some grown men would not do. As time went by we had some chickens, and ducks, and pigs. I learned to kill the chickens and ducks for food, but the pigs froze, and we buried them.

The most memorable thing about Dingle Hole Road was the school I attended. It was down the road and around the corner, and a way off, partially through a wooded area, up on a county route. Years later I would bring my children to the place we lived there on Dingle Hole Road. I trekked up to where the school was located; it was actually one mile from the school to our house. I went to school alone back then, because Regina and Paul were too young to attend. Regina, in fact, never went to kindergarten, because there wasn't one. Occasionally, Regina would come to the school sometimes and sit with me in class.

When I first opened the door, UNBELIEVEABLE!

The school was a one room schoolhouse. It was from first grade to ninth. First grade was up front on the left side. Second through seventh were behind first. Eighth and ninth were on the other side of the room. The front and right walls were all chalkboards. The chalkboards were black, and there was always some activity going on with the boards. The back of the room had a small, attached coatroom that also housed the wood stove. The toilet was just outside; it was a two-seater also, just like the one at home. There was no girls or boys room, just a piece of wood on a nail inside. A turn of the board locked the door. The outside handle was this little black latch. If you pulled on the door and couldn't open it, that meant it was occupied, except in the winter when the door was just frozen.

We had monitors in class, appointed by the teacher. They preformed a variety of tasks from keeping the fire going in the winter, to opening and closing windows in the summer. They also had helpers who were anywhere from first to seventh grade, monitors assigned jobs to the class; cleaning, sweeping, stacking wood, putting things away, or straightening out the books in the small library in the back corner of the room. Everyone, including me, had their chance at these chores. The school kids were like a family; we never fought much. If there was a spat, the teacher would fix it.

There was this one kid, Arthur, an eighth-grader. He was sort of small, but a head taller than me. One day we all had to go to the school Saturday morning for a shot. Arthur passed out before he got to the head of the line. I ran for the door, but my mother and the nurse caught me. It was worse by running, as everyone laughed at me. After that, some of the older boys would say, "Run, Al, Arthur looks a little pale."

We had the greatest time when a holiday came. On Halloween, the teacher would string donuts up across the room at the party, and then dare us to try to bite one with our hands behind our backs. He would shake the lines, and we had powder all over our faces. The biggest party was at Christmas; we would start getting ready weeks before the holiday. The teacher would start the singing lessons and practice the carols. The upper classmen would stand in the back, the lower grades in the front, all standing in the front of the small school room. My position was right center, the front row. I was one of the smaller kids. Our teacher would tell us to watch him. He would give us these breathing exercises. When he raised his wand, we would take in a deep breath. When he lowered the wand, we would exhale. This went on for a time trying to get the class to start all together. Then at last he raised the wand, holding our breath, waiting for the wand to come down. Suddenly Arthur passed out, right behind me. He fell forward, almost taking me to the ground with him. The teacher dropped the wand and scrambled to the front of the room reaching for Arthur. I was already crying and went to my desk. Arthur was quickly revived, and everyone was settling down. Arthur was short of breath and just lost it. The teacher could not convince me to return to my place in the choir. When I went home that night, I told my mother what happened. I didn't want to go to school anymore, or at least I surely didn't want to take part in the Christmas play. A few days later the teacher moved me a few places to the left in the choir, and I was back in, singing, one eye on the teacher's wand and the other on Arthur.

It never occurred to me what a great school that was; I had attended schools all over the country, some of them were good schools, in fact, most were good schools, but that one room school offered the best lessons in teaching responsibility and brotherhood. Our recess was like something you might only read in a storybook. The kids played together, first graders with seventh or eighth-graders. One game was the brownies and fairies, the boys on one side and the girls on the other, about forty feet apart. The fairies were the girls, and the brownies were the boys. "Red Rover, Red Rover, let so-en-so come over." And the other side would respond by sending that person running across the playground as fast as possible, trying to break through the other sides locked hands. It was never a bully game, no one had ever gotten hurt, not too badly anyway, and when I think of it now, what an exercise. Another game was like that one but played with a ball. It was played with one person throwing the ball to the other side. If it was caught, the thrower was taken. It had to be thrown high in the air. The side with the most players, when the teacher called us in, was the winner. The brownies didn't always win; those fairies were pretty good catchers. It was the school family, everyone watched out for one another. I was only a first-grader, and then second-grader, but I can't remember anyone fighting.

My brother Paul was a couple years younger than me. He didn't go to school with me, but sometimes I would bring him along, or sometimes he would just show up at the school door. The teacher knew Paul, and would admit him, tell him to sit quietly and draw something.

Now there were two children that lived near the school, a sister and brother. I honestly can't remember their names, which is quite ironic. The boy was about a year younger than me and didn't attend school. His sister was my age and was in the first grade with me. She had almost white hair, as did her brother, and I thought she was the cutest girl in New York, or anywhere for that matter. I was so shy; I would never say that to her or anyone else. One summer day, Paul, Regina, and I were walking down the road to the school; it was near the end of the school year, so mom said I could take them with me. As we approached the school, the two blonde kids came running out to meet us. The little blonde girl, began to swoon, "Who is this cute boy, pointing to my brother Paul. Regina did all the talking (as she was a talker). I was too scared to say anything. I just kept on walking. Paul always attracted the girls. He was like a magnet to the girls. Years later, when Paul finally started school, there was one incident. The school system in Phoenix finally centralized, and partly because my father complained, a school bus picked us up at our door and brought us to the central school in Phoenix. Paul was just a kindergartener, and near the end of school that year, something happened. On a Saturday, cars were dropping off kindergarten girls dressed in dresses with presents. They informed my mother that they were there for Paul's Birthday party. Forget that Paul was born December 1st, we had no way to entertain these kids. My mother was helpless; she could not even give them a glass of kool aid. When one mother came, she told her the dilemma. They both laughed, and the woman said that Paul told her daughter that Saturday was his birthday, and everyone was invited. I think the girls stayed and played for a while, and then their parents came and retrieved them. There were no cell phones, and we didn't even have a phone in the house back then. Some of the parents never knew there was not a party till they picked up their kids. Paul got a house full of presents! My parents were not mad at him. I think they were bewildered and surprised at his actions. They just shook their heads, and I remember my father saying, "And don't you try to pull a stunt like that again." Paul's reason: he had heard that another person in class had a birthday party and got a lot of presents, so he told everyone it was his birthday. The girls in his class took it as a chance to party with Paul. Paul's birthday wouldn't come for another six months, so he actually had two birthdays that year. Later Regina and I would say Paul was catching up to us by having two birthdays a year. Paul was always playing catch up or hooky or something through the years.

The Vanishing Babysitter

One afternoon mom and dad were going into town and left a young lady to watch us. She seemed quite capable. Mom told her where the diapers were for the baby, what to give us to eat, and they left. Everything went okay for about an hour, and then she told us she was going to pick berries just down the road. She took a small pail; it was one of those sand buckets that a kid would take to the beach, and she swung it by the handle. "This will do just fine," she said.

She led us out to the road. I was holding Johnny, the baby, and Regina had Maria's hand. The babysitter pointed down the road and informed us she had seen a patch of berries just past the curve. She said she would get them for an after dinner treat. There we stood, huddled together in the middle of that dirt road, watching the babysitter slowly stroll away, swinging the pail, occasionally turning around and waving to us. "Don't worry, I won't be long," she hollered back at us. We waved back, but didn't move from the spot she left us. Slowly she disappeared around the distant curve in the road. We began to reason together as to how long she might be gone. We weren't worried about the little sand bucket; we never played with it much anyway. The minutes turned into hours, and there we stood, as though frozen in the middle of Dingle Hole Road. We scuffed our feet in the dirt of the road, searching with our eyes to the end of the road. Little Johnny, was starting to get heavy, and he needed a change. The sun was setting against the trees in front of us, so we moved to the house, like a troop of soldiers holding on to one another. By the time we entered the house, we realized how dark it was getting. I scrambled to find a diaper and made a first-time change. By now Johnny was crying pretty good, and Maria and Linda were echoing their fears. Regina and I tried to light a candle but couldn't find matches. Suddenly it was dark, and we now figured out the babysitter was not coming back. We huddled in the kitchen area and Regina was bawling, Paul was setting somewhere on the floor near the bottom of my chair, the other girls were setting in the other chairs, also crying. I was holding the baby, rocking him back and forth, trying desperately to comfort him. Then a noise in the driveway alerted us to the return of our parents. They came in and quickly lit the oil lamp. The dim light displayed my brother and sisters huddled on the floor in the corner. My parents couldn't believe what happened.

Two things about that event are burned into my memory even after fifty-five years. One was us kids standing and staring down the road at the sunset peeking through the trees, hoping against hope to see the babysitter coming back up the road, and the dreadful helplessness of the darkness, with no parent to give light and comfort. After that we would talk about the vanishing babysitter. Years later I would hear the Gospel, how a savior went away but promised to return, and how men are waiting for his return. It reminded me of that road, and that sunset and how we waited. There are differences, but the way we waited, and the hope we expressed, is very much like the Gospel. The darkness when hope is abandoned is also like the Gospel message.

Father and His Quotes

Dingle Hole Road was my growing up time. I learned and remembered more things at that place than anywhere else. Even some of the words used there were etched in my memory. My father had certain statements or sayings to express his feelings. These expressions were designed to get our attention, and they did. If he and my mother went to the store, he would tell me, "Don't open this door to anyone, even if the president of the United States knocks." I guess it meant no matter how important a person is at the door, don't open the door. Sometimes when they got back I would say the president didn't stop by. My father hated to get mocked in any way, even if I was only kidding, even if I was only seven. "You want trouble from me? Keep it up."

"Keep it up" was another one, not just the words but the way he said it. It was a threat; none of us could joke with him. He could demoralize you with his words. My favorite phrase was, "I'll cut off your arm and beat you with the bloody end of it." Whenever he got mad at me, he would rattle off this expression. It was not just words rolling off his tongue; it was the ultimate threat. His finger followed his eyes, he looked directly at you, it was not a casual expression, there was no swearing, or cussing. "I'll cut off your arm and beat you with the bloody end of it." Sometimes when I was relaxing, or walking to school, I would think about just how he was going to cut off my arm. Would he use a saw, or a knife or maybe he would just rip it out of the socket. I was sure I wouldn't survive the amputation, so the beating would not hurt too bad, I would assure myself. Regina would snicker after he said it. Not to his face, but when we were out of sight and sound. She would rehearse the phrase with a joke. The threat was only directed at me; she was not threatened. After a while I got used to those words and realized it was an over statement, in a threat form. He really wouldn't cut my arm off, I thought, but I was good just in case.

With all my dad's faults, I can at least say he never cussed or swore in our presence nor did he ever have beer in the refrigerator. We never saw him drunk. He took us to church, and sometimes when he wouldn't go he sent us. He was a smoker; he smoked Camel cigarettes. Most of his family and friends smoked. When they got around the table and drank coffee, the room was filled with smoke. My father loved the holidays. He was like a kid at Christmas and Easter and when it came to Halloween. He would send us out trick or treating, when it was possible, and he would allow decorating during those times. On July 4th he would come up with some fireworks, again, when it was possible. One time when we lived in California, he got a hold of some fireworks and burned his hand quite badly. He was protective of us and would not allow us to wander around the neighborhoods wherever we happened to live. We didn't have time to wander too much anyway. He kept us busy all the time.

Pilgrim Mother

My mother was a tourist and a pilgrim. She had very little voice in where we would live or what we would do when we got there. She would complain to dad about conditions; he would say he was doing the best that he could. Sometimes she would take a job here or there to buy food for the table or pay the rent. We had plenty of hard times. Mom had to make do with feeding us. When the kids were little she often mixed water and syrup for a baby formula. She had to take all the hand-me-down clothing and make it fit us as best she could. She was never too proud to take a hand out if it meant food for the table. She learned to cook what she had; many times we had potato peeling soup. One time we had ketchup soup on an open hearth with black gnats that looked like pepper. Sometimes she cooked oatmeal and divided it to us for the only meal of the day. It broke her heart to live on the road, but she did so, always hoping things would get better. Too many times she had to start over. One time she sat on the curb with her little band of kids, all of us crying, not knowing what our next move would be. She worked when she could, in big factories, working with electric components, in a cookie factory in California, washing dishes, washing clothes, in restaurants; her desire to survive and care for her family was utmost in her heart and mind. Later when most of her children were grown and on their own, she raised the last two, Daniel, and Sue Ellen, by working in a hospital, as a nurse's aide. She did so for twenty years, retiring with a pension. She was a woman of great courage and faith.

Chores

At the age of seven, I was becoming aware of my responsibilities within the family. I didn't think what I was asked to do was out of place. In fact, I thought we were living under normal conditions. For example, I thought most people had no running water or electricity. Didn't most people in 1951 have outside toilets? Of course when I went to school, I knew some people had electricity in their houses, but they were the wealthy ones. I knew it to be true because they had several changes of clothes.

My father assigned me to the job of getting water. The well was in the front yard at the end of the driveway. It was a hole in the ground with a piece of plywood over it. There was no wall around the hole, like you might see on TV with a crank and a rope. Our well had a rope and pail. It worked by throwing the pail and rope in the hole, then pulling the rope up with care, standing a little away so as to not fall in the hole. In the winter it was especially difficult to pull water on the icy driveway. All our water came from that well, whether it was for drinking or for baths. It seemed we always needed a pail of water. When I didn't or couldn't do it, mom got the water.

In the spring of the first year, Dad started bringing old cars out to Dingle Hole Road. I think he got them from the dealers where he worked either fixing cars or selling them. The cars were junkers. We would gut them out and burn them, cut them up, and junk them. It wasn't long before I learned to use the torches to cut the motors, doors, and fenders off the cars. Dad would leave the car, with instructions. Mom and I would cut out the motors and burn the cars. Later we would load the metal and junk it. There wasn't a lot of that going on, just two or three times a month.

On one occasion the three of us were junking a car we had burned out the day before. We lifted one end of the body onto the old truck, and in the process mom cut her arm. It was a bad cut and needed bandaging. The sore became infected, and her arm was bright red around the cut.

She soaked her arm in warm water every day and watched the red line in her blood vessel rise closer to her shoulder. Finally the red line went down into the sore. There were no doctor visits to Dingle Hole Road.

One of my first jobs was to get water from the well.
I used the rope and pail method,
worked for me summer and winter.

Ma washed our clothes in one of those galvanized washtubs. She had a washboard and scrubbed the clothes back and forth, up and down on that board. It seemed like she was always washing clothes, and I was always carrying water. That old tub was either full of old clothes or used to wash us kids. Ma would put the tub on the kitchen stove and light a fire under it. We would put water into the tub and wait till it got warm. Then, starting with the girls, Ma would wash us two at a time. If the water got too dirty, she would dump it and start again, warming the water. Sometimes we washed on the stove with the fire under us. Our parents would wash in the tub also. We would be sent out whenever one of them wanted to bathe. With five kids, the cleaning process was ongoing. Before we moved out of that place, we did get electricity. I think we had a plug in the kitchen and one in the bedroom. It amounted to a couple of extension cords strung across the floor. We even had a TV for a while, which was an on again-off again thing. The big shows were *Bride for Today* and *Search for Tomorrow*. The programming would end with the national anthem. I thought it was great to have a TV; we would set around on the floor and were captivated, even by the commercials. Unfortunately, it was short-lived. When I would again get a chance to see TV, there would be tremendous change.

Country-schooling

My FIRST YEAR OF SCHOOL THERE, WAS IN THE ONE-roomed house near route forty-eight. As I said, this was one of the greatest times of my life. In first grade I sat right up front on the left side of the class. Behind me was second grade, then third, and so on to the back of the room. The eighth and ninth were on the right side. The teacher would lecture the eighth and ninth grade classes in the sciences, sometimes math, physics, or even English. The rest of the class would be left to studying, but some of us underclassmen couldn't help but get our ear into the teacher's study. When he would ask a question to the ninth-graders, we would wave our arms wildly in the air.

"See," the teacher would exclaim, "even the first-graders know this one." Then he would turn to us and, shaking his finger, tell us to get back to our own studies and stop trying to shame the ninth-graders. I really can't remember his name, but he was a firm, just leader and teacher. He kept the peace and always settled differences between the students. Everybody liked him. Once he was off and we had a substitute, a young man, tall and broad in the shoulders. The substood before us and warned us to be good, and he was nobody to fool with. He took a pencil and broke it in his fingers. We tried that after he left, and even our regular teacher couldn't do it. The sub was surprised after a few days at the orderly manner of the group. He thanked us for putting up with his inexperience and later told us he was a trainee from the college in Syracuse. One day our regular teacher gave the first-graders our spelling words. One of the words was "if," and he instructed us to write the word fifty times on our paper. Well, I was always trying to take a short cut and began by putting a column of "i's" down the page. I had just started on the "f's" when he caught me.

"Alfred, what are you doing?" he said. He took my paper and held it up and asked the class to help me spell "if." Every one in the class had to spell it. Then he asked me to go to the board and write "I will spell if all the way out." When I finished, after he helped me with the spelling, he said it looked great and to do it one hundred times on the board. I filled the front board and the side board, and it took me the rest of the day, but I could spell those words pretty well after that, and he never caught me taking that shortcut again.

Sometime into the second year there, the little school closed; it was something about consolidating. So I still walked down to the little one-room school-house, there I waited for a school bus, which took me to a two-room schoolhouse not far away. This school was just a little bigger, and there were two teachers, both women. I was in second grade.

Regina was ready to come to school at this point. She never went to kindergarten. Dad didn't want her to walk to the old school and wait for a bus. It took a while, but he got the school system to pick us up and take us to the two-room schoolhouse. There was less learning and more confusion there. The teachers seemed to spend more time arguing than teaching. Who had this and who had that, and where are the scissors, the whole thing seemed to be thrown together to satisfy the school system, and the kids were along for the ride. This fiasco only lasted to the end of the school year, and then Phoenix centralized. This meant the school had to pick us up at our door and bring us to the town school in Phoenix. The first day of school Ma took our picture standing on the dirt road waiting for the bus. Regina was all dressed up in her dress and fancy blouse, holding her lunch pail. I, like her, had a lunch pail, ready for third grade in the big school. The Phoenix school was a brick building, two stories (at least). When the bus unloaded us, we walked around to the front door and waited in line for the doors to open. While we waited, Regina got aquatinted with the girls her age. She was not timid when it came to talking. I, on the other hand, never said hello to anyone. If any of the girls wanted to say something to me, they would talk to Regina and she would tell me when we got home. I would always say, "Don't bother me with that." I was a bona fide introvert. I would stand aloof at school waiting for the bus. I dreaded the thought of someone coming over to talk to me. I never would stand in class and give a book report. In High School I was a loner. More than once I told teachers that I would take the "F" for the book report if I had to get up in class. When it came to girls Regina would always tease me. Because I wouldn't talk to them. As I grew I pushed myself to keeping busy and keeping my mind off the subject of girls. I did okay, it kept me out of a lot of trouble. It wasn't that I didn't like girls, I think I was afraid of them not really liking me, or what would they see in a person like me? I may have been a little insecure and shy, but I was also caught up my activities, and chores which were extremely time consuming when I was around eight years old.

I really got to like the school and the teacher. We always had assembly first; one of the teachers would read a passage from the bible, and then we would sing a few songs and finally "The Star-Spangled Banner" and the Pledge of Allegiance.

Once we got to our classroom, the teacher would always go over the date. This so impressed me! In all my life, up to this point, I had never thought about the year. I knew Monday and Tuesday, the days of the week, the numbers of the months, even the year I was born in, 1944, but I never thought about it until this teacher made a big deal about it. I was growing and becoming more aware of the world around me.

We never had much homework when I attended the one room school house. I think it was because the teacher realized most of the kids were farm people who were very busy after school. Now when the school system consolidated the rural children were bussed into the town. The teachers there were either unaware of the circumstances, or didn't care. In my own case, which was a little special because of our impoverished condition, home studies were very taxing. For one thing there was what I had to do when I got home straightaway from school. There was water to fetch from the well. Sometimes I would spend an hour just filling jugs and pans. Then what ever projects my father left me to do. Most of the time he was not there when I got home, and sometimes he would not get home till late in the evening. The other thing was the light problem. We had one main kerosene lamp, we had to use it sparingly. Mother used it in the kitchen and sometimes in the other room. It was often moved around from place to place. For me to read at dusk or dark was difficult to say the least. I know there were others with the same problems, and I often thought about men like Abraham Lincoln who lived in a log cabin and must have had the problem of trying to read in the dark. I needed help with some of the work and had to ask my mother, she was not too well educated herself, and had four other kids to tend to. She did the best she could under the circumstances. But I hated the idea of homework after a while, it was a burden and responsibility I was not ready for. One day one of my sisters tore the pages out of one of my school books. When I brought the book back to school and the teacher saw it, she was furious. She vowed I would pay for the book. She wrote a letter home to my mother saying she expected the money for the book as soon as possible. The next day my father went to the school and called the teacher out of the class, with the principal in tow. The class could hear the argument out in the hall, I was so embarrassed. Most of the barking was between the teacher and my father. I could hear the principal trying to calm the two, "Now let's keep it down," she was saying. When the teacher returned to the class her face was bright red. "Well, let's settle down now" she said, but there was not a sound in the room. Her attitude towards me after that was very formal, and she often addressed me as mister Luckette. She still gave me the same homework but we never paid for that book. On my part I never thought of it as we got one over the school, but we just didn't have any money. By this time my mother was pregnant for her sixth child. And my father didn't have steady work. There was just no money for anything except the bare essentials. If I had to describe the impact of homework on my life at that time, I would say it was like someone dropping bombs on our house or incoming sniper fire. It totally upset the whole household. My father never liked school and didn't go any further than sixth grade. If I had homework I had to do it on the sly. He calmed a bit with the other kids, but with me he always pressed the point that I had more important things to do than homework.

When I had children of my own I always made sure they had a decent place and time to study. I always took the time to look over my children's homework. I would always ask them if they had school studies to do before they got involved in other activities. I would look at the place where my son was reading a book one time, and remembered myself out on Dingle Hole Road, sitting in the dark just a few feet from the kerosene lamp trying to make out the words on the page.

Sometime during the school year of third grade, I was on recess in the schoolyard. It was a fairly small yard with a few swings and seesaws. The seesaws, as we called them, were long planks that we teeter-tottered on. The seesaws were close to the building. I had been playing in the back of the yard when the bell rang to call us to return to the class. As I was running to the door, I came upon the seesaws. Running along the side of the building, I passed one set of seesaws, then as I approached the second set, someone on the other side pushed down on the seesaw. My side came up, striking me in the left side of my face, hitting me in the eye and above the eye on my forehead. Down I went! The next thing I remember was the school nurse carrying me into the building. Then the strangest thing happened. I went unconscious and dreamt of a rough texture against my body, and then something smooth seemed to come and make me better. In describing the experience; the dream started with a small animal coming into my vision. As the animal passed before me I became frozen unable to talk or move a muscle. Then a rough texture would come in contact with my body. It rubbed on my arm, it became more aggressive and covered my whole body, I struggled to try to speak. I thought of how I could get away from the small creature before me. Then suddenly a smooth feeling came over my body. It took a while to erase the rough texture, but in a short time I was engulfed in this warm smooth material. The school nurse was noticeably frightened when I awoke, I remember telling her "It's okay now every thing is getting smooth."

After a while, the school nurse brought me home. She was very apologetic to my mother and left me on the couch in a half-conscious state. My head was swollen, my eye was closed, and I was dizzy and numb. Then it happened again, as though I were wrapped in a wool blanket, like one of those old green army blankets, and it scraped against my skin like sandpaper. I slid back and forth on it and in it. At the same time it felt like fine, hard, sharp gravel. Then suddenly, when I thought I could take it no more, it changed, and a smooth feeling came over me. Back and forth these feelings came and went as I lay on the couch. It was like a dream, one I could not stop. The rough and smooth were directly related to the accident. I saw the seesaw. It was a green board, and it came to my face, hitting me in the eye, then the rough, then the smooth. I dreamt this as I lay in the semi-conscious state. After the accident, for weeks and months I had that dream. Sometimes as I was just falling to sleep, this dream would come. The condition continued even after I was married. The dream always started with the appearance of a small animal, then a feeling of complete immobility. The rough texture which I came to bear in later years, then the final smooth feeling that enveloped my being. After I came to Christ, the dreams seemed to intensify and became horrible and upsetting. My wife knew about the dreams and would wake me when I began to moan. Then one day I described the dream to my minister. He told me the next time I had the dream, ask Jesus to go after the small animal and take it away. Well, I had that dream shortly after that, and I found it difficult to even say the name Jesus, but I did, and the animal fled the scene and

I immediately awoke. It happened again, and I repeated my plea, *Jesus help me, take this from me,"* after that the dreams stopped. I mean completely stopped. I had that dream for seventeen years sometimes two or three times a week. Now I don't even think about it, I used to call it my Dingle Hole Road dream.

My Hot Water Bottle

Life on Dingle Hole road was tougher as I got older. The winters were very cold. One day we went to a secondhand store, and I saw a hot water bottle for sale for a nickel. It was one of those reddish-orange rubber bottles with a plastic screw cap. I told my dad I wanted it and he balked, saying I wanted to waste his hard-earned money on that nonsense.

"What are you going to do with an old hot water bottle?" he would say. But I kept insisting, and Dad was determined to deny my plea. Finally, the store keeper handed me the bottle and said, "Here, son, take it home. It's on me." My dad agreed to let me have it at that price. Mom and dad looked at me then the bottle, and then they looked at each other and shook their heads. I remember all the way home dad berated me on the water bottle, but he was really drilling me as to what I had in mind to do with it.

When we arrived at the house, we hurried in and dad lit the stove with some old newspapers we had picked up in our travels that day. It took about half an hour for the kitchen to warm up. We had a woodpile to get the fire going, and then a few pieces of coal were placed on top to get it a little hotter. Over the fire was the reservoir; it was a copper tank that held some water, which was now just ice. The kitchen stove was the main piece of furniture in the house, especially in the winter months. It was almost all cast iron. At the base of the stove were these claw feet.

They looked like the paws of a lion; rusty, black iron. On one side was the oven, with a huge door that would not stay up by itself. Dad had rigged it with a piece of wire so ma had to unfasten it when she wanted it opened. The other side of the front of the stove had a set of doors, one above the other. This was the fill and ash doors, and above these doors the reservoir sat. The top of the stove had these round plates that sat into the surface of the stove. The lifter was a small handle that fit into the plates to remove them to load the wood or coal in. The top of the stove had this kind of a hutch; I guess to keep food warm, although we never had any food left over to keep warm. Then there was the stove pipe. It went straight up out of the back of the hutch, and made a left turn to the chimney on the other side of the room. As you entered the kitchen, the stove and pipe completely dominated the scene. I would say it was almost mustard yellow, but it had black blotches with some rust.

Regina knew I was up to something.

Ma was hurrying to heat some food, but she had already put the water on for coffee. Dad was the only one that drank coffee then, and ma knew that came first. We were all huddling around the stove; the little ones were whining about the cold. Dad always hollered for quiet, but Ma never said anything. She would put her finger to her lips and put on a scowling look as to warn us to hush. The room was fairly dark as light came from the fire in the stove. The air vent in one of the doors was always open. We had a kerosene lantern, which was lit near the sink. This was what I was waiting for all day.

As soon as the water in the reservoir got hot, I filled my hot water bottle. It was a stealth operation; I took it to the bed and slid it beneath the covers. In a little while I would be basking in the heat of the hot water bottle secretly. Dad had forgotten about the bottle. He was drinking his coffee; Ma had poured out a portion of tomato soup to each of us, and we quietly dined. Regina knew I was up to something but had also forgotten about the hot water bottle. As soon as I finished eating, I said I was going to bed. Paul and Regina both slept in the same bed with me, so I wanted to make sure I got to my spot before them. Ah...I was right, the bottle had warmed the bed where I slept. I hugged the bottle and drifted off to sleep. In the morning, mom was hollering for me to get up, but something was dreadfully wrong. I was freezing cold. By morning there was usually no heat in the house till Ma got the fire going. But this time I was colder than I ever was. I pulled the covers away, and there at my feet was my hot water bottle, frozen hard, with my feet on it. The bottle froze and kept me cold all night. My plan had backfired. When my father learned what I did, he confiscated the bottle and tried it himself with more success. I never got the hot water bottle after that, but I will never forget the disappointment of the frozen bottle the morning after. It was common in the winter there for any glass of water to freeze up over night if left out. We didn't have a refrigerator and didn't need one. The whole house was one soon after the stove died down.

We got electricity in the second year there. It was in the form of an extension cord from the pole near the road to the house. It ran a small radio that Ma loved. We would lie in bed at night and listen to the hillbilly music until we would fall asleep, and it also provided power for a few lamps. The house was small, so two lamps pretty much lit the whole house. I remember one song they played every night. I can't remember the words exactly, but we called it the billboard song. It was hilarious, about torn signs on billboards. Back then it was all we had to entertain us.

Well-digger

The property next door to our house belonged to the same man that owned our place. It also had a small house on the property, even smaller than ours. It was vacant, but dad made a deal with the owner, who was a real estate dealer. The deal was that dad would rent the place out and take care of the house. There was one problem: the property had no well. Again my father came to the rescue. He agreed to dig a well on the land. Early Sunday morning we picked a spot out behind the shack and dug a round hole about three feet in diameter. We dug and dug till dark, and then dad said we could quit for the night. On the way back to the house dad told me to start in with the digging the next day right after school. When I got home the next night, Ma reminded me about the hole. I dug all that night and got down about two feet. Dad never came home till late or early in the morning. I usually didn't see him till the weekends. He must have been digging some while I was in school, because the second day the hole was down about four feet. During that week I went straight to the hole after dinner and dug till dark. By the weekend, we were down to about six or seven feet. We dug all weekend, and by Sunday afternoon, it was too hard for me to shovel the dirt out of the hole. Dad got a bucket and rope and let it down the hole, and I would fill the bucket, and he would lift it out and dump it. We had this rickety old ladder with broken rungs let down into the hole. When I looked up from the hole, the top looked like a little saucer. Dad was standing at the edge of the hole smoking his cigarette, with the rope in his hand. I would dig on one side, and the other side would cave in a little. Then I would dig out the caved in side, and the other side would cave in. At one point the bottom of the ladder was covered by a cave-in.

This whole scene continued into the following week, and to my surprise, my father was home when I got home to finish the digging. He supervised my digging from the top rim of the hole, pointing to where I was to dig next. The hole got pretty deep. I think he said it was over twelve feet, but the cave-ins were more frequent, and one time a whole wall came crashing against me, trapping one of my feet. He scurried down the ladder and freed me, then hurried up the ladder again to his position with the rope and bucket. One Saturday morning I went down the ladder to find about six inches of mud in the bottom of the hole. The ladder had sunk about a foot in the mud. I could not dig anymore. We thought the water might rise in the hole, but it never did. We threw the bucket down in the hole but only got a little mud in the bucket. Dad took a ruler and measured the hole; it was almost fourteen feet deep.

We left the hole for a few hours, and when we returned, the walls had caved in dramatically. He measured the walls again, and the depth was about nine feet. He abandoned the project and ordered us to stay away from the hole. I was totally relieved to not have to go back to the hole. I was always frightened of small or enclosed places. That hole was a nightmare, having to climb down into the hole and look back up at the small patch of sky was unnerving. I would think about the hole and having to go there, maybe like some people think of dying and having to be buried. I felt like a great weight was moved from me. I acted real disappointed when dad said we have to give it up, but in my heart, I was rejoicing. Even to this day I can see that small patch of sky, as I'm standing by that ladder looking up and signaling dad to lift the bucket.

Dad got a bucket and a rope and let it down the hole
I would fill it up and he would lift it up and dump it.

The broker rented the little house out anyway to a group of Native Americans. They only stayed for about a month and would be gone for most of the day and return at night to sleep. One morning Paul and I went over there early to find them all sleeping on the floor like a bunch of over-sized logs. The little shack was no more that twenty feet long and ten feet wide, and there were over fourteen people living in it. I got to know a few of the men, and one of them, an older gentleman they called grandpa, caught a large snapping turtle and had the women cook it up. I had never had turtle before, but I thought it was pretty good. Grandpa showed me how to catch turtles with a stick and cut their heads off. One day they came home early and had a big party; they cooked a large hog on an open fire outside. Later that day one of the women came to our door with a big plate covered with a tray top. She gave it to my mother and said they wanted to share their bounty with us. My mother took the plate and carried it to the table and took the tray off to find a pigs head cooked and with an apple in its mouth. My mother screamed and threw the tray in the air. When she finally calmed down, she covered the tray and set it back over on the counter. We sat in the kitchen and watched the Native Americans dancing and singing around a fire in their front yard. For some reason my father got home early that night. It was almost dark, and my mother was crying. She showed the pigs head to him. Dad turned to me and said, "After dark, take that thing out back and bury it."

I did, even as I could hear the party continue on into the night. The next day the neighbors had left. They never returned to Dingle Hole Road. Later in life I learned the head of the pig was considered a treat to some people, a delicacy reserved for honor. Those Native Americans had given us the best they had; they honored us. We were poor, stupid people and didn't know any better. We buried the treasure instead of enjoying it.

The animals

We acquired a few chickens, ducks, pigs, and a couple goats over one summer. One of the goats was a nanny, whom we milked for a while. We would use her milk on our oatmeal, and sometimes just drink it straight. It was a very rich milk, and had an unfamiliar taste. The other goat was a Billy goat. He was very large and had big horns that just slightly curved from his head to his back. Dad had him on a rope inside a fenced area. Sometimes Paul and I would climb the fence and tease the goat. We would try to grab him by the horns and see if we could wrestle him to the ground. One day Ma gave us some potato peelings in a paper bag and asked us to feed the goat. Usually we would slip the food under the fence and the goat would drag the paper in and eat. This time we thought we would have some fun with Billy goat. Paul went around behind the goat and distracted him while I entered from the front. I carried the bag up and dropped it, when the goat turned, Paul grabbed the rope and began to tug on the goat so he could not chase me. Suddenly the Billy goat turned on Paul. Paul dropped the rope and began to run for the fence. The goat charged Paul at full speed with his head lowered and horns straight up like a straight back chair. Paul was screaming and running, and the goat was closing in. I ran for the fence as I watched the action. The rope holding the goat broke, and at about four feet from the fence the goat caught Paul. Those huge horns hit Paul right on his back side and lifted him off the ground. For a second it looked like he was riding on the goat's horns, but the goat stopped at the fence and Paul continued to fly over the fence into the pigs mire. Paul fell face first in the mud. My mother heard his scream and came running. She saw Paul as he flew over the fence. We all began to laugh hysterically. Even Paul thought it was funny.

Paul was a tireless kid. He could run for hours. He would chase rabbits in the back yard, and catch them most of the time. He would hold the rabbit by the ears, carry it to the house and let it go. I think he caught the same rabbit several times, it was a game the rabbit may have been in on. I never caught a rabbit.

We had pigs we planned to butcher in the fall but never did. When winter set in the pigs froze to death and Paul and I dragged the dead pigs to the unfinished well hole out back and slid them in. In all we put quite a few dead animals in that hole. Once a neighbor shot our dog in the driveway. That dog went to the hole also. That old well hole was our official burial site. So in the long run digging the hole did serve some purpose after all.

Chicken suit

My father liked to dress up; he was Italian. He had a rose cashmere suit and a Stetson hat. When he dressed up, He wore rings on most of his fingers. He would wrap his folding money, (which wasn't much) around an empty thread spool and hold it together with a rubber band. He would put it in his front pocket. It bulged out in front of his pants; you knew he had a wad of something in his pockets. Sometimes he would just wrap paper then a few ones around the spool. I think the people he hung with at the time must have inspired him to do those things. When he dressed up, it meant he was going out, not us, not Ma and him, but he was going out. It was as if he lived two lives, one with us, and another in town as a wheeler dealer. When dad dressed up, it meant he would not be back till early in the morning.

When it came time to kill a chicken for food, Ma or I would have to do it. One afternoon I was ordered to kill a couple of the chickens for our dinner. Dad was dressed in his suit and standing in the yard. My cousin Bob was with us that day; Bob lived with us quite a bit. When he heard I was going to kill a chicken, he offered to do it. He said he saw his grandfather kill chickens by ringing their necks. So he grabbed one of the chickens and began to twist the neck. The chicken squawked and Bob dropped the bird at his feet. "I think I'm going to be sick," he said. The poor bird's neck was broken! It hung to one side as it ran to and fro in the yard. I grabbed the axe and chased the bird down and chopped off it's head. The chicken began to run around squirting blood everywhere. Then it happened: the chicken came right at my father and squirted a stream of blood across his cashmere pants. He was furious, and he ran to the house and changed his pants. Ma was soaking the suit pants in cold water. I was the culprit, and dad hollered and hollered and threatened to beat me with my arm if the stains didn't come out. Ma called me in and told me to help her. I think she wanted to get me out of the way. She said to me, "Good for him! Stay in here and wait till he goes." He did leave with another suit, not as fancy, but he and Bob rode off as I hid in the house. I couldn't figure how I was responsible for the blood on his pants, but one thing about my father was, if something went wrong, it was always someone else's fault.

The Bald Neck Rooster

Dad liked to watch the roosters fighting. He even introduced new roosters into the population for that specific purpose. One day he came home with a bald neck rooster, one of the ugliest roosters I had ever seen. He had huge spurs and was taller than any of the other roosters. Dad released the bird in the yard, and in a few minutes the bald neck bird began to pick on one of the bantam roosters. The bantam was king of the yard and took no guff from anyone. Ten minutes into the war, dad intervened and grabbed the bald neck rooster and put him in the cage. The bantam had almost killed the ugly bird. Dad was hollering at the bantam about how much he paid for the bird, as if the bantam knew what he was talking about. I nursed the bald neck back to health over the next few weeks, but he was never released. Dad sold him to a neighbor. I remember him telling the neighbor about how we had to keep the bird penned because he was apt to kill all the other roosters if he was released. The neighbor was just like dad; he wanted that killer bird. Dad bragged to us later about how he sold the bird to the neighbor. When I went around to the neighbor's house later, I found he had the bird caged just as we did. That rooster was so ugly the neighbor could have charged people to view it. The neighbor must have found out the same thing we did. The bald neck rooster looked bad, and scary, but he could not defend himself to save his life. I learned a great lesson from that bird, life was full on Dingle Hole Road.

The baldneck rooster was taller than any of the other roosters. And twice as ugly.

The Trailer Trip West

I THOUGHT MOVING OUT IN PHOENIX WAS A BIG DEAL, BUT dad had an even bigger move in store. Dad wanted to be a lawyer, but he had only a sixth grade education. So he applied for a high school equivalency regent's exam, which was given at Syracuse University at the time. He was told that he had to start with a high school diploma. He studied a few books they gave him, and he passed the test with a pretty high grade. Somewhere he acquired these law books, which he was always reading. He went to take the bar exam, but they told him he couldn't take it with an equivalency diploma. I sometimes wonder how my life would have been, if dad had been allowed to take the bar exam in New York. Anyway, he found out he could take the bar exam in Mississippi and become a lawyer there.

My little brother Johnny was born in February of 1951; I can still remember when I first saw him coming up the driveway in my mother's arms. He had a yellow tint and cried like he was being tortured. A few months later we were loading our belongings into an eighteen-foot trailer and a 1941 Cadillac to trek out to Mississippi to live.

We settled in Jackson, and Regina and I attended school there for a while. We lived in a trailer park, in that eighteen-footer; Mom, Dad, and six kids. We had all our possessions there; the trailer was so packed there was almost no floor space. One night my dad wanted to hear the fight between

Rocky Marciano and Archie Moore on our radio in the trailer. A great storm was raging, and the trailer was rocking back and forth. We listened to the pre-fight announcements, and just before the fight started, our power went out. Dad scrambled to the car to hear the fight. Ma and us kids were huddled together, the little ones were crying hysterically in the darkness. After a few minutes, Dad came back in the trailer soaking wet. He said by the time he found the station, the fight was over. The next morning the park was flooded. The park owner had a monkey caged up near her house, the cage almost totally engulfed in water, and the monkey had almost drowned. The town was just about all under water. I later tied the storm to the Marciano\Moore fight. We got in only one marking period at school when dad decided to leave Mississippi. He had this idea of going to California. He sold the law books going through Texas. It was a long, slow, trip with some schooling and many flat tires, but we finally reached Los Angeles.

California

The sun just seemed so hot; it reminded me of the kitchen stove back on Dingle Hole Road, when it was blazing with kindling wood and how it would burn your face if you got too close. There was just no place to hide from the heat. We landed in a trailer park near the town of Glendale. Dad backed the tiny trailer into a spot next to a lush plot of greenery. Each spot had this area about the size of the trailer. There was rich, green grass and a few small trees and bushes. Some areas had small benches and chairs where people sat in the mist of their garden hoses. Our trailer had a rounded top, and the back seemed to slant back like one of those old, fast back cars. Years later a manufacturer would come out with a trailer called the streamline, which had a stainless steel body and were quite expensive. We had one then, but it was not a streamline. It was not stainless steel, and it was not expensive. We lived in cramped quarters. Dad let the water run almost constantly on the little patch of greenery next to the trailer. I had a new job here; keep the grass green and move the hose from one spot to the other.

Dad got a job at the airplane factory. He was a riveter building planes. For a while it even looked like we may start living like normal people. Ma made our lunch for school and off we went. The schools out there were bigger, and the kids were richer. There were those who made fun of the tiny trailer we lived in. Learning Spanish was mandatory. When we came home with study papers with Spanish words, dad objected to our learning any language but English. Any second language should be Italian, which he spoke fluently, but he wouldn't take the time to teach us. Ma didn't speak Italian, nor could she understand the language. I remember saying the Spanish word for pen. Dad quickly corrected me, giving me the Italian word, and admonishing me to say it correctly. Two things happened I remember quite well while we lived in this first park. My father burned his hand badly playing with a firecracker one 4th of July. Some of the neighbors brought him to the hospital, and his hand was bandaged for weeks after that.

The other thing happened at his job; a rivet that hit him near his eye, injured him. He went to the doctor a few times and missed some work. The factory gave him a settlement, and that was the end of the job. I think he got about seven hundred dollars. It was enough for him to strike out on his own, and he did. I often wonder what might have happened if he had put that money in the bank and continued working for Lockheed. Maybe he could have retired with a nice pension, and some of us kids might have even gone to college. But it was not in the stars; we had another course to follow.

The first trailer park was a clean, neat place, every shrub and blade of grass in place. The driveways and roads were smoothly paved with blacktop. It was an upper-class park, if there was such a thing. Our trailer was the oldest one there and stood out not only because it was the smallest but the rustiest. In fact, I don't think there was another trailer with rust on it. When the day came for us to leave, we had the trailer and the old car loaded with our stuff. The neighbors stood out by their trailers watching us as we pulled away, and I could see them looking at each other shaking their heads, as if they couldn't understand our leaving.

Watering the grass was my new job, but we never

had a lawn mower, or a goat to eat all the grass.

We landed in a second park; this one was larger but clearly not as upscale as the first. Dad and I went to see a man about a larger trailer he had heard about from someone in the park. It was a fifty-footer, by eight feet wide, the front corners were quite rusty, and the bottom was coming apart at the seams. We made a deal and swapped the trailers. We got some angle iron and repaired the seams in the front of the trailer. It was really nice to have a home with a little breathing room. We changed schools again, this time we were in Burbank. I was in the fourth grade by now, and some time went by. This park marked my change in schools at least three times out there, so I finished third and started fourth in California.

This second school was the most memorable to me, maybe because of its unusual format. It was made up of about twenty quanset huts and about four rows of five huts. They were attached to each other at the ends. They looked like airplane hangers. Each hut was self contained with toilets and a small kitchen area.

The day at the school started very similar to the one I attended in Phoenix, New York. The teacher would call attendance, and then rain or shine we would stand and file out under the sun port to sing "The Star-Spangled Banner" as the flag was raised in the schoolyard. Everyone held their hand over their heart and every one sang; it was a solemn event. We then went back to class where the teacher would select a chapter from the Bible kept on her desk. I didn't have the materials all the time, and the teachers had to make due for me to participate in class studies and homework assignments. It was while I attended this school I contracted shingles, a sickness that made me very ill and in a great deal of pain. I remember my schoolteacher bringing me home and telling my parents of my problem. She gave me this new coat, because the weather had turned cold. It was a beautiful coat, not only warm but colorful, and I loved that coat. It was one of my only possessions. As the weather warmed, I was forced to brown bag it, as dad would say.

I didn't want to give up wearing the coat even when it was really too hot to have it on. I would say, "It's a little chilly this morning, I think I'll wear my coat." Regina would roll her eyes and say, "Dad, Alfred is going to wear the coat again." She was embarrassed to see me wearing the coat in seventy degree weather. Her friends in school asked her if I was nuts. I guess I was a little overboard with it, but I knew that next year if we still had the coat, either Regina or Paul would be wearing it, and I wanted to get all I could from that beautiful coat. We never got rid of clothes until they were impossible to wear, or completely worn out. Every thing was passed on from hats to shoes. As I remember, that coat mysteriously disappearing shortly after I stopped wearing it. I think my father sold it in his second hand store.

The Gypsies

In the center of this park was a large cement block building. It held men's and women's rooms and a room with washing and drying machines for clothes. The park was huge, and the owners had a small store in the front along the road. The driveways and roads in the park were dusty, stone, and sand. Some roads looked like they may have been paved at one time in the past but were in great disrepair. One night a noisy group of people came rumbling into the park. We heard the screaming and hollering, and it sounded like they were partying and having a good time. In the morning there were about seven new trailers lined up in one end of the park not far from our trailer. They were Gypsies. I had never seen or heard of those people before. My mother told me to stay near the trailer. The Gypsies settled in and began to wander around the park. Some of the women had small babies, and they would put chairs out along the block building and sit and nurse the young ones. This was right across from our trailer. Ma would tell Paul and me to busy ourselves and stop gawking at the women. I guess we didn't have to watch them, because dad kept a pretty good eye on them anyway. The young Gypsy girls would spin in their dresses to show everyone their lack of under-wear. They would stand at the doors of the men's room and try to entice the men passing to allow them to tell their fortunes. They would ask to hold their wallets, then stick the wallet down their blouse front and either run or play with the wallet till they got the money. There was a constant complaint to the management about the Gypsies. They really knew how to get things from everyone. At night the Gypsies would have these little bonfires near their trailers. They would play guitars, banjos, and the ladies would dance with tambourines. Many of the people from the park would gather around. It was another way for the Gypsies to get money from the men. We would sit in our trailer and listen to the lively music late into the night.

One night about midnight we were awakened by the Gypsies as they came roaring into the camp. They were screaming and hollering. They had just come from the local carnival, where many of them worked. They quickly hooked their trailers and sped away. Suddenly it was quiet. I laid in bed and listened; maybe they were only going for a ride somewhere. We never saw the Gypsies again. I remember the next day, walking in the places where the Gypsies trailers had been setup. I walked around their fireplaces, kicking at the ashes. I was standing where I would not dare be for the last few months. It was a dream, the force of these people on my young life, which made me and my siblings cower with fear, a fear of the unknown. Our parents feared them. I didn't know why, but I felt it. The Gypsies just seemed to fly away in a whirlwind in the night.

The Yellow Bike

The custodian of the park was an older man in his forties. He took care of the plumbing in the washrooms. Sometimes he would just clean up around the park. One day he came to me and asked if I would like a bicycle. He had recovered one found in the park that no one claimed. I guess he had it for a while and wanted to clean out a work shed he used for keeping park equipment. It was a twenty-eight inch bike, and it was so large I could not get on it from the ground. I grabbed the handlebars; I had never had a bike! "Thanks," I told him and walked it home.

He started right in at saying how badly I was painting the bike.

Now, the old bike was quite rusty. It was an old English-type with hand brakes on the handlebars. There were no cables; the grips had steel rods that ran down to the wheels to brake the bike. I never knew if it was a three speed or five speed. I never got that far with it to find out. I would climb the stairs at our trailer door with the bike on the side and mount the seat. I could only reach the peddle on the top of the stroke. I'd push off and peddle as hard as I could down the road in the park. After about one hundred feet, I'd loose control and dump the bike, and then walk it back to the stairs for another trip. I was afraid to go too far and even play with the bike too long, in fear of what my father might do if he knew I had the bike. After a few spills, I put the bike under the back of the trailer on its side and covered it with some cardboard.

My dad finally discovered the bike, but to my surprise he allowed me to keep it as long as I didn't ride too much, which meant never when he was around. Dad always had a job for me. At this time I had no idea what he did for a living. I only knew he was gone at intermittent times. Ma took a job at a cookie factory and would come home with a package of these Oreo-type cookies nightly. I couldn't wait to get home; I'd uncover my bike and bring it up to the steps, then down the road. Each time I'd ride a little farther. Down at the end of the road there lived a few families of Native Americans. They sort of stayed to themselves, except a few of the kids would roam the park. One of the boys would come up to our end to pick on Paul and me. He was a few years older than me and really pushed me around and mocked me as I rode my bike.

One day, not long after I got the bike, the park custodian came strolling up to our trailer with a gallon can of paint and a large four inch paintbrush.

"Say, Al, wanna paint that bike?" he asked.

"I finished painting my shed and have this paint left over; there's enough to put some paint on that old frame if you'd like."

"Sure," I replied right away, taking the paintbrush from his hand.

He set the can down, and after telling me to just throw the brush away when I finished, walked back towards the front of the park. The paint can was better than half full of a bright yellow color. I thought at the time the best way to paint the bike was to cover the rusty spots. After a while of painting, I found it necessary to paint everything but the tires. I painted the wheels, the fenders, the frame, the handlebars, and I was working on the chain and pedals when the bully approached me. He started right in at saying how badly I was painting the bike. He was complaining about me painting the handlebars and was trying to take the brush from me to prevent me from finishing the chain. We struggled for a moment, and then he got the brush. I quickly grabbed the can and dumped it on his head. Paint ran down his face, into his eyes, and all over his shirt. The boy began to scream and cry and ran towards his home at the end of the park. I stood there for a minute, and then began to wipe the brush. My bike had fallen over; I was in the middle of picking it up when I saw three women walking briskly up the road in my direction. They were older, heavy-set women, big, blanket-like shawls were draped over their shoulders. They had stern looks, and I ran for the trailer. I entered and went straight to the back of the trailer, passing my mom on the way. A moment later there was a loud knock at the door. I could hear the ladies screeching in and unknown tongue and mom asking what they were saying. After a while they stormed off, and my mom came to the back of the trailer and asked me what was that all about. I tried to explain, but the more I said, the worse it sounded. "Wait till your father hears about this! Boy are you going to get it," she said.

Later that night I had to explain it again to my father. He took my side, but the bike was all done. It couldn't be ridden anyway with all that paint it just seized up. We left it under the trailer when we moved out; it remained there under the cardboard. Regina and I would joke about the yellow bike for years after that. We left that trailer there when we moved again, this time to another park in a vacant trailer. The new trailer was about the same size as the last. The schools seem vague to me now, but I remember the names of the schools were after the presidents; Roosevelt, Jefferson, and Washington.

A Trip to Vegas

My father had a garage in Burbank by now, and I was the cleanup boy. He was painting cars, but he didn't let me paint anything. There was a man who came in and did trim work on the cars and trucks. He was real good with a paintbrush. He would trim around the wheels and hoods. Dad told him to keep the brushes away from me. During this time dad got a forty-eight Oldsmobile convertible. It was a real beauty, chrome all over, with spotlights near the doors. He decided to take us to Las Vegas for the weekend. We had no trouble till we got almost to the town line in Vegas. The motor quit; it was making a noise for a few miles, then there was one big bang and the end. We had it towed to a garage where we found out the engine threw a rod. We spent most of the weekend in the bus station. We slept on the benches in turns. We even played the slot machines; they were everywhere. Regina and I had a few nickels and were playing a machine in the back of the bus station. I was winning big time. I had my pockets full of nickels, so I said to myself, *I'll never have to work again*. I thought I was rolling in dough. Regina did not fair as well, but she was ahead in her winnings also. That night we piled into the back of the bus headed to Los Angeles. I was on the backseat, Regina at my side. She told dad that I had money in my pockets. Dad asked to see the money. I tried to downplay it, but Regina kept nagging, "Alfred's got a lot of money." Finally my father turned to me and insisted on seeing exactly how much money I had in my pocket. I counted it out slowly, It came to a little over five dollars in nickels. He confiscated the money and berated me for not coming forward with it earlier. Five dollars was a lot of money in 1952. You could buy a coke for a nickel.

I gave Regina a dirty look; she smiled and wagged her head. "Dad, Alfred's going to hit me," she chanted. "He better not get smart if he knows what's good for him," came the voice from the direction of where my father sat. The rest of the ride home was spent in dreamland. The whole fiasco trip was a nightmare. When we got back, it was only a few weeks and dad closed the garage.

Shoe Business

Dad's new thing was a cut-rate store in downtown Burbank. He began to collect used furniture and clothing for the store. He had stoves and refrigerators stacked to the ceiling. One area had racks of clothing and shoes. This was my back-to-work mode. Every day after school I would go to the store and sweep and hang clothes on the racks. Sometimes I would help him move the heavy furniture around the store.

Then there were the shoes. One day my father made a deal with the president of a shoe factory. He agreed to give all his "seconds" to the store. "Seconds" are shoes with some defect in some way. I remember the day they were talking about it in the back of the store. *How many of those could there be,* I thought. *How many mistakes could they make?*

Then one day shortly after that meeting, Dad took Paul and me to a vacant lot not too far from our house about a mile away. He explained that he wanted us to come here every day after school to sort shoes. While we listened, a huge truck came to the spot. Dad motioned for the driver to back up. The truck backed to the middle of the lot and dumped about ten thousand shoes right there on the ground. The pile must have been ten or twelve feet high; black shoes, brown shoes, oxford shoes, ladies and men shoes, all mixed together. Dad picked up a couple of the shoes, holding them in front of him. He explained how we should look for matches. The color, the size, rights and lefts, all these things had to be considered. Then we put the matched shoes on a box. We began to search the pile, meandering around the huge dump of shoes. After a few minutes I found a match, one of the shoes was scuffed on the toe, the other had some noticeable defects also. After a short time, dad left us and said he would return later on. Paul wanted to throw the shoes around and play on the pile of shoes. He climbed to the top of the pile and threw himself down, tumbling over and over till he reached the bottom. After a while I grabbed Paul and told him I needed his help. "This is serious; we need to find some matches before dad returns," I admonished him. We searched all afternoon and succeeded in finding a few matches. When our father finally returned, he seemed somewhat pleased and told us to get over to these shoes every day after school to sort them.

The pile must have been ten or twelve feet high, black shoes, brown shoes, oxford shoes, ladies shoes, men's shoes, all mixed together.

The walk from school was only about four or five blocks to the shoe pile. It was in a nice neighborhood with small, ranch-styled homes lining the streets all around the empty lot with the pile of shoes. Our lot was on the corner; it had tall grass and some small shrubs. There were fresh sidewalks out front. This was a far cry from the dirt road back on Dingle Hole Road, yet it was so much the same, a place where I worked. At nine years old, I now was the foreman on a sorting shoes job. I had been pressed into service, I had a good resume, I had worked the farm, I carried the water, I beheaded the chickens, dismantled the cars, and a host of other chores that must have put me in such a trusted position. I was in charge. Paul, on the other hand, was a six-year-old who just followed me from school to the shoe pile. He liked to pass the time throwing the shoes and playing cow-boy on the shoe pile. I did get him to put the brown shoes in one pile and black in another after a while, so every day we went to the shoe pile and sorted till almost dark. Dad would come with his car and pick us and the sorted shoes up and bring us home. By the time we got home we were hungry and tired. My sisters had already eaten hours ago, so Paul and I would set alone at the table and eat, then be off to bed.

One day as Paul and I were at the shoe pile sorting shoes, we saw this elderly woman strolling across the street in our direction. She was carrying two mugs in her hands and calling to us. "Yoohoo, boys, I have something for you," she called to us. Holding the handles tightly on the steaming cups, she smiled brightly as she approached us. Her offering was a warm chocolate drink she called Ovaltine. We sheepishly refused at first, telling her it was not allowed for us to accept it, but when she pressed the offer, Paul took the drink and began drinking. I took the other and thanked her for the drink. The kind lady explained how she had been watching us come and sort shoes. We thanked her again and went back to our sorting shoes. So every night the lady across the street would bring us a mug of the hot drink. We had become anxious in expecting the drink each night as we sorted shoes. Then one day the lady came across the street with no drinks in her hands.

Paul looked up her way and said, "Oh, oh, no chocolate."

I looked up a little disappointed. She approached us with her usual smile.

"Boys," she started, "come across with me to the house. I have the drinks and a sandwich for you pre-pared; I'm sure your dad won't mind you taking a break and having something to eat."

This was a serious matter; our father would kill us if he ever found us in a stranger's house. I told the woman it would be impossible for us to go over there. Our dad would not allow us to go. She kept trying to persuade us and would not relent. Finally, Paul said he was hungry and going to eat, and he stood by the kind lady indicating his position in the matter. What could I do? The only thing that could be worse than going with the woman would be let-ting my little brother go alone. This was the way I reasoned it out and finally relented into going. She took us by the hand, one on one side, one on the other, and took us across the street. My heart was pounding. What if my father found out? Once in the house, she led us to a table in her dining room. The table was set with sandwiches on plates and napkins neatly set on the side. And right near the sandwich were the mugs of hot Ovaltine. Her table sat near the front window. We could clearly see the pile of shoes across the street. We munched the sandwiches and sipped the chocolate. My eyes never left the picture across the street of those shoes. I could see Paul was enjoying the meal. We didn't get any chocolate like this at home. I was thinking he would tell Ma about it, but he didn't. No one ever found out about the angel God sent to feed us.

The shoe thing went on for about two months. After a while I guess dad had other things to sow. One thing led to another, and we found ourselves on a train heading back to New York. Dad had gotten himself into trouble with the law. One of the lawyers paid for the trip for mom and all of us kids. Dad had to remain behind. Before we left, I had gone to my fourth California school in just under two years. My last memory was our living in a cabin. There was a group of cabins in a community; our cabin was centered in the middle and was one of the largest. Most of the families were Mexican. They were friendly, and there were a lot of kids. One of the fathers, a husky man of Mexican decent, had a pair of boxing gloves and would get the kids to box. He watched us pretty close, and no one ever got hurt too bad. Sometimes he would get other fathers to help out. He also organized a baseball game for the kids, which we played in the dirt parking lot in front of the cabins. He brought a little of my childhood out. At first I shied away from the playing, but the man who coached us kept sending his kids to get me. Finally I got the nerve to go. I enjoyed it but felt a little guilty for having fun.

The train ride was like a dream. We slept on the seats; the backs went down into small beds. The scenes were sometimes breathtaking. We would look at a mountain range for hours. The big stop was in Chicago; the train station was huge. There were soldiers everywhere. We had to trek through the station to catch another train and we barely made the train.

Back to Syracuse

WHEN WE REACHED SYRACUSE, THERE WERE SOME problems in getting adjusted. I think we had help from the welfare in getting a place to stay. Ma had six kids and no means of income. We ended up living with a family on Crouse Ave. in Syracuse. We had an upstairs apartment. I started in school at Washington Irving grade school, and by now I was just finishing fourth grade. With only a few weeks to go, I had to do a lot of studying to pass into the fifth grade.

Now, the Allen family lived down stairs. There were three boys and a girl named Ruby. Freddy was the youngest of the boys. He was about my sister Regina's age. He had been stricken with polio when younger, and it left him crippled. He had braces on his legs and walked with crutches. Freddy was home-schooled. He was a diabolical imp, a spoiled brat, and I'm being kind. Freddy did what he wanted. If he didn't get what he wanted, he would throw a tantrum that could be heard for a city block. The first time we experienced it, we were upstairs. Freddy was screaming and throwing things around. The next day my mother asked what happened; Freddy's mother sheepishly told her about Freddy's temper. He always got his way.

After a while we got to know Freddy, Paul and I would take him with us when we went somewhere. Once in a while Freddy would want to go up to the university and roam around. One day we happened on a garbage cart. It was a green cart with two large wheels and a smaller wheel in the back that swiveled to let it turn. We removed the cans and put Freddy in the cart. It had a neat handle that ran across the back to push the cart along. Over the next few months we used the cart to carry Freddy with us. The people at the university knew we had the cart but never said anything.

We were without dad during this time. There was a kind of easiness to my life. I'd go to school and afterward watch a little TV downstairs at the Allen's. On the weekend we would go downtown and see a movie at one of the many movie houses. You could go to the matinee for a dime. All the kids would go, and sometimes the theatre would pass out bags of popcorn for the kids. It was a great time. Then one day I got home from school, I started up stairs, and Mrs. Allen caught me and said I should wait downstairs for a while. I shrugged her off and darted up the stairs. I opened the door, and there, standing in the center of the room was my father. Mom was sitting on the end of the bed. He was crossing examining her, and he almost ignored me. He glanced my way and continued his questions. Ma was crying. I stood there for about a second and he looked back at me. "Haven't you got something to do?" he said. I turned around and went downstairs. Mrs. Allen told him he could not stay there.

The next thing I know, we were living in Manlius Center. I was finishing fourth grade, and after a short summer, started fifth grade. Fifth grade was kinda hard for me; I had trouble with the multiplication tables; those times tables were impossible to learn. I had a little tablet, and on each page I wrote the times tables. Page one were the ones, page two were the two's, and so on up to the twelves. I lived with that tablet day and night. I also was a fairly bad speller.

I couldn't spell to save my life. I had to work extra hard at those two things. Now, history, geography, and science were easy for me. I could read a book and remember it like I was reading it during a test. But I couldn't do it with spelling and the times table.

At this point, I think it is interesting to bring up a coincidence. While attending the school at Washington Irving, in the fourth grade, a third-grader named Frances Parker attended the school at the same time. When we moved to the Minoa school district, Frances' family also moved into the school district. I never consciously remember seeing or meeting her at Washington Irving or at Minoa back in 1954. It wasn't till I returned to Minoa some eight years later that I met her through my sister Regina. After high school we dated and married in sixty-five.

Manlius Center Store

M<small>Y FATHER HAD A STORE IN</small> M<small>ANLIUS</small> C<small>ENTER</small>. I<small>T WAS</small> a small ma and pa type store. A few canned goods and candy. He sold some refrigerated goods like milk and sodas. A bread truck came every day with fresh bread. He was always telling us the food was for the customers. We ate a lot of macaroni back then. Ma would cook three pounds, and everyone got one helping. We lived in a house next to the store; sometimes Regina, Paul, and me would set by the window and count the cars as they passed. It was a very busy area. We even developed a game from the passing cars. With paper and pencils we would pick colors and makes of cars, then as the cars passed, we would mark each time a color or make came by. Sometimes one of us would be winning on the colors and the other on the make. We got pretty good at naming the makes of the cars. Back then a car was either a Chevy, Ford, Dodge, Plymouth, Chrysler, Nash, or one of the other GM cars. The colors were pretty basic also. I remember how we loved that game. Later when we were on the road, we played the game as we rode in the car, sometimes from morning to night. It was our video game of the fifties.

Hepatitis

Something went dreadfully wrong during my final months in the fifth grade. I became deathly sick and was in bed for about two weeks. Regina came down with a bad cold, and my mother convinced my father to let her take Regina and me to the clinic in Syracuse. I was so weak I could hardly walk. When we got to the clinic, we were told to sit out in the hall with the crowd of people already there. The doctor came out to take one of the patients in. He glanced at me and then did a double take. He approached my mother and asked if I was her child. She quickly responded with a yes but asked if he could see Regina first because she had such a bad cold. "Not today, madam," he answered. "I'll be seeing him first." He took me in the examining room and ordered me to sit across the room in the corner on a small stool. He was speaking to my mother, and at one point she raised her voice and said no way. What I could not hear was what the doctor had in mind for me. When he first saw me, he noticed a yellow tint to my skin. He said I would have to be held for observations and that I could not be allowed to leave under any circumstances. Ma told the doctor that her husband would not allow me to stay there. The doctor called my dad, and I guess dad got pretty scared because he came in to town. By the time he got there, I was already in the hospital. My parents came in dressed in long robes and masks; Seeing them like this was frightening, What was wrong with me? At first I was in a lone room with a thick glass on one side. I remained there for about a week. After that I was moved to a ward where there were others suffering with the same disease. There were about twenty in all, and many of them were from Syracuse University. We all had hepatitis, a disease of the liver. We were fed big meals with milkshakes and fruit nectar. I never ate so well, but it did little good. I grew weaker and weaker as the time went by. There was an epidemic of the disease in the city. Everyone that had contact with me had to have blood tests and shots to boost their chances of not getting the disease. At first my father refused the shots; he was chicken. When they told him he might die, he took the shot. Ma told me this years later. One by one the men and boys in the ward were taken out. Finally there were just two of us left. I had been in there for about three months. The other boy was about my age, and he was called Poncho. After the end of the second month, I started to feel a little better. Poncho and I would talk about his home and brothers and sisters. We were not allowed to write letters or have our parents get too close to us. No schoolwork came in or went out. I was informed while in the hospital that I would have to repeat the fifth grade. It didn't seem to matter, as the doctors told my parents, I probably would not survive. Even after I was released, the medical staff told my father I would not survive to twenty-one.

It was in my fourth month that they wheeled Poncho out. He said good-bye and we promised to meet after we got out. There I was, alone in the ward. I took up drawing pictures of faces of people and cartoon characters. I spent my last days there reading and watching television. Then one day a nurse told me I would be going home soon. I was so excited. When my mother came in I asked her, and she said in a week I would be going home. My skin had lost most of its yellow tint and was a milky white from being sheltered from the sun for about four months.

My mother came in early with some new clothes the day I left the hospital. I had gained a lot of weight. When I went in I was about seventy pounds. The nurses weighted me at ninety-six the day I left. None of my old clothes would have fit, but they had to be destroyed anyway. The new sneakers were a size bigger also. Mom slipped them on me and tied them up. One of the nurses came with a wheelchair to bring me down to the front door. I refused and said I could walk down. When I jumped off the bed, I fell flat on my back. I could not stand. My legs would not hold me up. I was in shock! What had happened to me? Then I was told I would have to go slow with standing, as my strength in my legs would slowly come back. When I got home I asked my mother if she got Poncho's address, as I wanted to write him and tell him I was home. My mother changed the subject, saying that I could do it later when I was stronger. I kept asking and she kept hemming. Finally she told me that Poncho didn't make it. I thought she meant he was still in the hospital. Then she hugged me and said Poncho didn't survive the disease. He had died just a few days after he was removed from the ward. I later learned that almost all the people in the hospital ward with me died from the disease.

Gumball Caper

The little store my father had was still running, and the gas pumps out front were still working as well. Gas was sixteen cents a gallon, high test was a penny more, but who could afford high test? We had one of the first mini-marts and didn't know it. I do remember my father making coffee and selling it to the drivers who stopped for gas. Our station was full service. That meant I had to check the oil and clean the window for each customer. But you have to remember, they were paying a good price for the gas. Sometimes I think about the businesses we had, others during that time frame and later successfully had businesses just like the ones my father started. Some of them became very famous and successful like the idea of having a mini mart with a gas station. When we were in California, we had a cut-rate store very much like the Bargain outlets, or the Salvation Army stores that sell used clothing and furniture. Later My father had a restaurant with a 15 cent hamburger, one of the first in New York State. My mother pumped the gas when I was in school. When I got home, after my recovery from my illness, I became the gas attendant. We would stay opened till ten o'clock, and I again had a conflict with school work. My pumping gas and watching the station was imperative.

One day I heard my father hollering in the store, and I ran in and found the old wooden floor covered with gumballs. The gumball machine was lying on its side with the glass ball broken. Pennies were everywhere. My father grabbed me by the arm and began swatting at me while my mother stood by. I tried to plead my innocence, but there was no chance. Dad was asking me why I broke it, how did I break it, and if I realized what that thing cost? While he was shaking me, Paul came walking in. My mother saw him first and signaled to my father; they were both now staring at Paul. I glanced around as I felt my father's grip loosen on my arm. There Paul stood in the doorway, his mouth full of gum, his lips wet and dripping from the gum. Both cheeks were so full he looked like a chipmunk with his mouth full of nuts. Then I looked closer. His pockets were also swelling, full of pennies. He had so many pennies in his pockets his pants were hanging on his hips. He stood there chomping on the gum and holding his pants. We were all speechless for a moment, and then my father asked him where he got the gum. *Boy, was that a dumb question,* I thought, but remained silent. Suddenly, I was off the most wanted list. I was dispatched with a warning to be careful around the store. Paul was never reprimanded, but he had to return the pennies. I think to this day that because my father punished me for the crime, he felt he couldn't punish

Paul for the same crime. He did study some law; I think there is something about double jeopardy.

Paul was my little brother; I didn't mind taking a spanking for him. I never brought it up to him after that. Paul was defiant to authority. Things that I would never think of doing, Paul would do. Some-times I would think, *How did he ever think he would get away with that.* Maybe he never thought about it. Like the time out in California, he had this girlfriend, who was about his age. He and she were sitting on the steps of the store in the front of the trailer park where we lived. They were eating a couple of those small cakes and drinking sodas. Regina and I came upon them and asked him where he got the money for the soda and cake. The little girlfriend beamed back to us and said, "Paul got some money from his dad."

"Dad gave you money for soda and cake?" I asked.

"No," he replied, still munching on the cake. "I got some money out of his wallet while he was sleeping." I was terrified; when dad discovered the money gone, he would kill us. I asked him why he would do such a thing. He assured me dad would not miss one lousy ten dollar bill when he had two more in his wallet. Paul was about six years old then. Later when my dad found the money missing, he lined us up and questioned us till he found the truth. The cross examinations were terrible; dad could have been an interrogator for the army. When he got through with you, you felt like someone dragged you behind a car for forty miles. Anyway, Linda or Maria finally squealed on Paul. Paul had tried to hide the fact that he took the ten, and Regina and I would not squeal on him, but he was bragging to my little sisters about the change he had in his pocket. One of them told dad. Paul had this thing about having money in his pocket. He just loved to put his hand down in his pocket and jingle the change. If anyone gave him money, he would run to the store and get change for his pocket.

Boy Scouts

Well, because I spent so much time in the hospital, I had to repeat fifth grade. I guess someone could have tutored me through it, but there were some mitigating circumstances. It was difficult to get supplies in and out because of the worry of contamination. I was completely quarantined. Then there was the question of just who would chance catching the disease to teach me. And also there was the notion that I may not survive, after all some did die there, so why burden me with what may turn out a worthless effort. In any case, I repeated fifth grade. I found myself in a peculiar spot. Regina was now in my grade, and school was all of a sudden easy.

Shortly after starting fifth again in Minoa, we moved to East Syracuse. We lived in a lower flat on the south side of the railroad tracks. I went to Heman Street School, and I was in the sixth grade. I had many memorable times there; it was the first school where I had to defend myself physically almost every day. I will not go into detail about the fights and scrapes Paul and I got into. I will, however, relate an incident or two that occurred there. The first started the day Paul and I got a note from gym class offering all male students an opportunity to join the Boy Scouts. Now I was never excited about joining the Boy Scouts, but the Boy Scouts played baseball after school, and I liked the idea of playing a little ball. We took the notes home to mom. The note said we needed two things to join the Boy Scouts. One was fifty cents and the other was our parent's signature. We finally got our mom to sign, and she somehow came up with the dollar for the entry fee. I was so excited I was going to be a Boy Scout. So after school, Paul and I met and went to the gym with our money and permission notes. There were a lot of boys waiting in line to sign up. The coach sat behind a table in the middle of the room. One by one the boys came to the table with their fifty cents and permission slips. They each signed the clipboard on the table and the coach shook their hands and welcomed them to the Boy Scouts. Paul was standing in line just ahead of me; we were not the last in the line, and before long there we were. Paul reached for the clipboard and dropped his note and money on the table. The coach stood and looked sternly at us; he pointed his finger at me and said something about "your kind." I told him we have the fifty cents. "Sorry, boys, we don't need your kind in the Scouts," the coach said. Paul and I walked out while the other boys were laughing and chuckling.

Heman Street School sat at the end of the street. Walking to our home was a straight shot to the bridge and around the bend to our house. We walked along think-ing what we would tell our mother. What had we done to have the coach ban us from Boy Scouts? I really wanted to play baseball. We would watch the boys assemble and the coach bringing out the bats and balls for the games after school. We would set on the sidelines and wish we could play. When the opportunity arose, we thought we would finally get to play. But our hopes were smashed. We didn't have the best of clothes and lived in a basement apartment, our parents were probably getting some sort of assistance from the county, and we got free lunch because of that. We were just kids and didn't understand what we'd done. Paul was madder than I was, so he said we should do something.

We plotted and planned all the way home. When we got to the house, we returned the money and told our mother we were too late to get in, but next year we could try again. She bought it.

The next day we informed the boys at school that any kids wearing a Scout uniform to or from school would become a target for a fight. Some of the boys said they weren't afraid and would wear the uniform anyway. I got out of school and started home. Paul had caught a Scout in the second block and tore off his shirt. Meanwhile, I saw a Scout leaving the school behind me; he dared me to fight him. He got a good shellacing and also lost his shirt. I got into three fights the first night, and Paul had a couple also.

The Scouts told the coach, and he told them not to fear the Luckette brothers. At first he advised them to double up, walk home by two's. When that didn't work, the coach informed the principal about the matter, excluding the part, of course, about him refusing to let us join the Scouts. We were held after school till all the Scouts went home. No one in East Syracuse wore a Scout uniform while we lived there. We would leave the house early in the morning and wait for the boys to come to school; they would carry their uniforms in bags. Back then it was like wearing an army uniform; the boys loved to wear that outfit.

The second incident was a more personal thing. My father took us to an auction and bought a bicycle for fifty cents. The bike was an old English bike with two flat tires. It laid around for a couple weeks, and I finally found a way to get the tires fixed. Dad wouldn't let me ride it very far, but one Saturday I went over the bridge with the bike. I got my mother to let me go to the Sacks store in East Syracuse on Main Street. I wandered around the store for a while just to say I was there, and then came back on the bike. I was heading home over the bridge; the road curved sharply to the right, and the bike went out from under me and I slammed into the curb. My hand almost immediately began to swell. It took about a month before I could use my hand; of course my father checked it out and said I had a bad sprain. Much later after, about forty years, I learned I had broken my thumb, and it never healed properly.

The Dog Pound

Our next move was into Syracuse on Beldon Ave. The building was an old dog pound, two stories high, with a yard in the back closed in with a cement block wall. Downstairs was a garage area and a basement with cages much like jail cells. In the corner was a mechanical elevator. It could hoist from the basement to the garage floor with a rope, much like a chain fall. The basement had a gas chamber, still intact near the elevator. The ASPCA would gas dogs and load them on the elevator then hoist them up and truck the bodies to the dump. Our apartment was upstairs; a second apartment was also upstairs, the second being more of a studio apartment. There was a small apartment downstairs with one bedroom. One end of the upstairs had a large room with cells; it was like a small jail. The whole building had a distinct smell of dog. My father had a garage downstairs on the main floor. It took weeks to clean the place. It always smelled like dog. A friend rented the small apartment upstairs, and the downstairs was rented to a lady with a couple small kids.

Teacher's Pet?

I went to Prescott school. The first day Regina and I showed up at the school and went to the principals' office. We introduced ourselves and announced that we were in the same grade and wanted to enroll. We were already a month or so into the school year. The principal, at first started to give us a hard time about our parents not being with us. When we explained that they had four others to enroll in the primary grades, she relented. She took our names and made a few calls to our last school. Regina and I sat in the principal's waiting room, a place I would frequently visit in the future. Finally she emerged with a few papers and directed us to the hall just outside her door. There we met two teachers, Miss Kaiser and Miss Malotoney. Miss Kaiser was a woman in her late thirties. She was well dressed and wore a bright lipstick that seemed to go well with her gray skirt and white top. Miss Malotoney was quite a bit older, probably in her sixties. The teachers greeted us with a smile and handshake as we were introduced by the principal. Then suddenly, Miss Malotoney asked what our names were again. She said she thought the principal said Al Luckette, and she muttered something under her breath about it not being possible. By this time I noticed Miss Kaiser already had Regina by the hand and had pulled her around almost behind her.

"Who is this boy," Miss Malotoney asked again, pointing to me but holding her finger close to her body so as to not contaminate it by the air around me.

"This is Alfred Luckette," the principal proudly announced. "Is your father's name Alfred?" the teacher asked me.

"Yes," I replied. "I'm junior."

The teacher screamed and grabbed for Regina. For a few seconds it was like two women at a basement sale. The Principal got between them and finally asked what the problem was. Miss Malotoney again pointed at me this time and her finger was shaking.

"I had his father, and I won't take him."

The principal was talking to the teachers as Miss Kaiser slowly backed down the hall with Regina.

"I'm sure it will be just fine. Now, take him along to class," the principal said, patting Miss Malotoney on the back.

I looked up at Miss Malotoney; she looked at me and said to come along. She turned and walked ahead of me. When we came to the class door, she opened it and waved me in. She told me to stand in the front of the class while she got me a desk. She went to the back of the class and pushed one of the empty desks to the front. She butted the desk against her desk and said in a very stern voice, "You sit there and don't move till I say so."

I quickly took my seat, I thought, *Boy what did I do now.*

Miss Malotoney was a pretty good teacher; she was old school, and I do mean old school. She wouldn't take any sass from anyone. I was always very quiet and seldom hung around with anyone. I was usually the first to my seat in the morning and never spoke in class. I was kind of shy and extremely introverted. Miss Malotoney would ask me if I was really who I said I was.

One day I was setting at my desk with a little free time, drawing, as I loved to draw. The teacher was busy correcting the homework and was not paying attention to my staring at her, because I was drawing a likeness of her face. Before too long she caught my eye and got up and came around the desk, quickly grabbing the paper from my desk. She looked at the paper and looked at it intently, and then she looked at me, then back at the paper. She never said a word; she went back to her desk, and put her head down holding it in her two hands. The drawing was before her on her desk. Again she looked at me and again at the paper. Then she called me to come around to the side of her desk. She put her arm around my shoulder and quietly told me she was sorry for treating me the way she did.

"You are not like you father," she said. "You are a fine young man. Now let's move your desk with the other students."

She got up and rearranged one of the rows to include me. The class was somewhat bewildered by her actions as was I. After we were all settled, she excused herself and took my picture with her. After a few minutes she returned to the class with a bright smile on her face. It was the first time I could remember her smiling. Later that day before the end of class she told the class to check the bulletin board in the hall before we left school. When the final bell rang, I quickly went to the hall bulletin board in the main hall. There was a crowd of kids from both fifth grade classes gathered around. I pushed my way in, and there it was, my picture of Miss Malotoney. She had put my picture up on the board in the hall.

Miss Malotoney and I got along pretty well after that. She told me about how my father acted in her class. And how he was hit with a rubber hose by the principal, and how he locked the principal in his closet and jumped out of the second story window. How he was expelled from sixth grade and couldn't return. The teachers back then were afraid they would get him back in one of their classes. Well, when Miss Malotoney heard my name, she figured I would be another troublemaker. This story is about me and not necessarily about my father, but I have to relate some of the events in his life that directly affected how I lived and what happened to me.

We lived, as I said, on Belden Avenue. The place was built like a fortress. The back yard looked like a scene from the Alamo. Paul and I played a lot of cops and robbers because of the jail cells in the building. My mother got a job at GE and took the bus to work most of the time. My father did work in the garage and sold costume jewelry.

The rent from the apartments paid our rent. I know my father rented the apartments and collected the rent. The woman downstairs was always cleaning her apartment. The smell of bleach and a strong pine scent was always present when she opened the door. She had a boyfriend who came around two or three times a week. He was a flashy dresser. One day the lady and her boyfriend were arguing; we could hear them through the floor. Dad waited for a while and finally went downstairs and threw the boyfriend out. He never came around again, although the lady said she was still going with him. The lady living upstairs in the small apartment was a friend of the family. Her boyfriend was one of the DeJohn brothers. He was a prize fighter. I never really knew him as a fighter though. He just seemed to be a big, kind man with a good sense of humor. One time he was taking the TV out of his girlfriend's upstairs apartment, and coming to the stairs he dropped it and it went crashing down the stairs all the way to the bottom.

We heard the commotion and came out in the hall to find them arguing. She was complaining about the TV. He bought her another TV and that was the end of that.

We were going to church at this time, my mother and us kids. Dad would go once in a while. The church was over on West Onondaga street. It was a Pentecostal church called Grace Assembly. We had attended the church even when we lived out in Manlius Center, but not as frequently. My Sunday School teacher was Brother Coots. I loved church. I liked the minister, and I liked his preaching. When we lived in East Syracuse, the church had a visiting evangelist who worked with the young people. He challenged us to invite a friend to church. The one who invited the most people would win a prize. This evangelist would draw a picture as he told a bible story. The prize was the picture he drew for that night. He also had a yardstick wrapped with candy bars, and that was the grand prize for whoever brought the most for the week. Well, I brought East Syracuse to church, not all but three bus loads. Every night there were some different people. The pastor had the busses from the church waiting in East Syracuse every night of the campaign. I won every picture and the candy bars. I kept the first picture, and every night after that I gave the picture to someone who brought a friend. The candy bars? Well, I had a big family. The best part is what I really got from those meetings. I was moved by the messages and was sure that God was going to be with me in whatever I would do.

Garage Worker

DAD GOT A JOB FIXING THE BUSSES. I REMEMBER UNCLE Louie coming over to the garage and helping him out. One of the buses needed a valve job. This required removing the head and grinding the valves and lapping them into the block. The engine was an old flathead, so a lot of the work had to be done right on the engine as it sat in the bus. I was working on the bus one night, sitting on the front of the engine, using a lapping tool to face the seat in the block. Dad was right beside me, up on the fender. When a man came into the garage and approached us. Dad was holding a ballpeen hammer. The man said he wanted to see Alfred Luckette and produced a paper from his jacket pocket. He extended it to my father, and asked if he was Alfred. The man kept prodding the paper at my father's arm, and my father kept trying to avoid being touched. It was an awkward few minutes, and then the man produced a badge and said he was a deputy sheriff. That was it, my father jumped off the bus with the hammer in hand and told the sheriff to get out, pointing the hammer at the open overhead door way.

The sheriff said, "You're served; I touched you with the paper."

Dad was furious; he ran at the man who turned and began to run for the door. The hammer left his hand flying towards the sheriff. It must have missed him by only inches, hitting the edge of the doorway.

The chase continued into the street where the sheriff made it to his car and sped off. Dad had the door handle and finally had to let go. The next day a man showed up at the garage about five at night. I was still working on the bus. He was a very heavy man in a late model car. He stood in the car's doorway and called to me. I got down and went to fetch my father. When we came downstairs, dad told me to go back to work, that this man was a friend. I watched them talking in the driveway. Then the man pulled a big wad of money out of his front pants pocket and peeled off some and gave it to my father. I found out later the man was a gambler named Joe D. He gave my father money to pay the bill and get a lawyer. I didn't know what it was all about, and never found out what the paper was served for. I only knew it was for a bill he never paid. Dad had known Joe D. for years; he worked for him when we lived on Dingle Hole Road. Joe D had card games at his places, and I was told most of the city police dept. owed him in one way or the other. One time my aunt was trying to get a drivers license and had failed a few times. When we were visiting her she told my father about her troubles. He took her permit to Joe D. He signed his name on the top, and the next time she took the test she passed. My father said she hit a parking meter and couldn't u-turn, but she still passed. I guess a lot of people were afraid of Mr. D. Years later someone ran into him and killed him on Genesee Street in Syracuse. My father said it was a hit and run.

Restaurant Business

THINGS WERE CHANGING IN MY LIFE AGAIN. MY FATHER opened a restaurant across from Prescott school in 1957. It was a small place with a counter and a few booths. The young kids flocked in every night. He sold about twenty cases of soda daily. He introduced a fifteen cent hamburger, add a dime and you got French fries. The jukebox was always going. At first I didn't have to do much, mostly just the heavy stuff like stacking cases and bottles. Before long he got into an argument with the building owner over the weight of the soda cases on the floors. Dad wouldn't pay the rent, and he had to move.

We moved from the dog pound to a house over on North State Street, and he opened another restaurant down the road on the other end of N. State St. By now I had changed schools again, going to Salina School on LeMoyne Ave. on the city's North side. The school grades were from fourth to sixth. My brother Paul went to Franklin over on Court Street. I only went there a short time, but it was there I graduated from sixth grade. During that summer I really got acquainted with the restaurant business. I think before we get into that, there are a few loose ends to tie up.

THERE ARE SOME PICTURES in my youth that have very little foundation. I'm sure everyone has bits and pieces of their childhood implanted in their brain that are hard to give a name or put a time to. I'm no exception to that. For example, I lived in a place called Pier Point Manor, and I must have been about four years old. We had a radio that sat in the living room against the wall. It was a tall thing with skinny legs. We would set around it and listen to the music that came from the large speaker in the front of it. It was like a piece of furniture, all wood. My mother liked country music, and we became accustomed to it. When my sister Linda was a little baby, mom would hold her in her arms as we sat in a little semi-circle listening to the hillbilly station. Another time when I was even younger, when we lived in Louisiana, I remember having this sailor outfit, and my mother taking me for a walk down the street. I ran ahead of her and into the path of a car. I laid on the ground and put my feet up as to stop the car. My mother was screaming, and the car's brakes were also screaming. It stopped with me under the front bumper, my feet up on the undersides of the car. My mother was crying and screaming. She thought I was hurt, but I reassured her not to worry, that I stopped the car with my feet.

My father had some contacts with unsavory people at times, and he came into things either given to him or loaned to him, or he made a deal. One time we had a jukebox in our home. It was one of those old types with the colored lights. The top was arched like a church window. It played the large 78 records. One of the records was Elvis, singing "You ain't nothin' but a hound dog." We played that record over and over, and thought it was a foolish song. This was when Elvis was first starting out, and he wasn't quite as popular as he later became.

We moved a lot when I was young. I never became too familiar with my surroundings as some young people do. As I said earlier, I didn't have friends, and if I became acquainted with someone, it wasn't for long. In a few places we had my father's nephews living with us, Tom and Bob Fortino. They were teenagers and would fight with each other all the time. I remember my father breaking them up and hollering at them. They would apologize and continue to argue. Bob, the younger, would give no ground, and sometimes they broke something in their fight. I thought they were my older brothers for the longest time. Tom would pick me up and carry me under his arm, sometimes running, and I would scream. Bob liked to pick on me. My mother would holler, "Bob, stop teasing him!" Bob would laugh and say something to the effect that I was teasing him. But generally we really got along well, and as I said, I thought they were my brothers.

My sister Maria was the quiet one. She was born after Linda and before Johnny. When we lived on Dingle Hole Road, we would be setting around the table eating, and Maria would always fall asleep at the table. She would be eating with her fingers, she was only about two, and she would drift off to sleep, sometimes sleeping and still eating. Regina and I would take the plate away from her, and she would be picking the table with her fingers and bringing them to her mouth in the motion of eating. I remember one time putting peas in front of her when she was sleeping. She hated peas, but in her sleep she ate them just fine. Maria would follow us around like a little shadow. She never got into trouble as a kid; she was like my mother, just along for the ride. As I stated before, this book is about Alfred Jr., but my family was there. Maria took a lot of abuse from our parents as we got older. I'm not a psychologist, but perhaps frustration on the part of my mother was sometimes vented towards us kids. Maria, for a while, took the brunt of it. For that I was and am truly sorry for Maria and what she experienced.

Now, in some families, one may be designated as the pet. If our family had one, it was princess Linda, or queen Linda as we sometimes referred to her as. She was pampered and protected from the rest of us. She was never too far from my mother's skirts. She was different, and didn't like to get dirty or play ball. We would have to coax her to play with us. Even when Maria was the baby, ma would be holding Linda, and Maria would be left crying on the floor. Linda played it to the hilt, never relinquishing her right to the throne or allowing ma to move on to the next in succession. Linda turned out okay anyway, a little spoiled, but okay.

Being the oldest, I was the babysitter and responsible for any wrong doing they may have done. My father would always admonish me to watch my sisters and brothers. When they did something bad like write on the walls (when we had walls), I would always be brought to the front with, "Why aren't you watching these kids."

OUR SECOND RESTAURANT WAS, as I stated before, located on North State Street in Syracuse, New York. The building must have been a motel or small hotel at one time. There were individual rooms in the back along a long hall. The restaurant was two large rooms with a separate kitchen area. Our restaurant was called Lucky's. The front room had a counter with stools, a few booths and tables. The back room had booths around the wall areas, a large dance floor, and of course a jukebox with all the latest songs. This was 1957, the golden age of rock. Elvis, Little Richard, Jerry Lee Lewis, Fabian, and a host of other rock stars drove the kids from their homes to the dance floors. That jukebox was going from 4 pm to 11 pm every day. The jukebox man would have to empty the cash box and refill the coin returns every afternoon.

The only thing I remember serving there was hamburgers, french fries, and lots of sodas. Once in a while someone would order a steak and fries, or steak and home fries. We would go through about fifty pounds of hamburger a day. Ma and I would make the hamburgers in the kitchen at night; we would scoop a little meat with an ice cream scooper onto wax paper on the table in rows, then we would press the meatballs down into patties with the underside of a plate. Every patty was the same size. Then the patties would be stacked in the refrigerator for the next day's business. The process took about an hour. The second chore was the French fries, which we made at the time of the order. But the potatoes were washed and put in a large pot. In the morning before school I would start the grill and put the home fries on and make the coffee. Ma would come in and serve breakfast after I left.

By now I was in the seventh grade at Grant Junior High, which was located over on Grant Blvd. on the city's northeast side. It was a large school for the times. It covered grades seventh through ninth. It was about a mile and a half from the restaurant to the school. The gym class was so large I never got to meet the coach. He wanted every one to wear gym shorts, which had to be white. Dad refused to buy the shorts. After a few exchanges between my father and the coach, it was clear that the coach was upset with my father. He lined us up and announced that there were some here that had no shorts, and we were getting failing grades for not having shorts. His solution was used shorts, which he had brought out and piled on the gym floor. Then he ordered anyone who needed shorts to sort through the pile and find a pair to wear for gym. He never approached me personally or ever spoke to me. He spent most of the gym class in his office after roll call and short inspection.

My job in the restaurant was short order cook, I was only five feet tall so it worked well for me. I also was the dish washer. I had real clean hands!

My cousin Don attended the school with me for a while. He would never wear the shorts for gym or do any school work at all. He had an attitude that he was in prison. He talked to the other kids in class as though the teacher was not there. If a teacher sent him to the office, he would get up and go, and turn to me and say, "I can set down there as well as here." Another kid in some of my classes would set by the window and cut his name into his arm with a razor. Every day he would work on his arm. After a while he had "John" scratched into his right arm bicep. Most of the time after that he had it bandaged and wrapped with gauze. As for me, I was the tattoo man. I would draw pictures on the boys arms with colored ink pens. I got pretty good, and quite a few had my drawings. One of my favorites was a ribbon with their name on it.

The format of the school was set up very loosely. I never really knew if I was passing or failing. But I must have been passing, because when we moved, my grades went with me, and I was passing. After school I had to get to the restaurant, every afternoon I had to prepare for the evening crowd. I spent a lot of time doing dishes, which I really enjoyed. It was a time by myself. I enjoyed working alone, and still do, back then I would bask in the job, totally engulfed in the task. If someone spoke to me I would not even hear them. We had these big three bay sinks, one tub had dishes soaking, the other was for rinsing. The third tub was for glasses, we must have had two or three hundred glasses. Sometimes I would spend a couple hours washing just glasses. Around four I would sweep the floors, and wipe the tables. My mother was pregnant again for my brother Dan. She worked right up to the day she went to the hospital to deliver. She had this fetish for crushed ice. She was constantly chewing ice. She would take a towel and wrap some ice cubes in it and beat the towel with a claw hammer. She kept the hammer under the counter, and no one could touch it. When she started making crushed ice that hammer had to be where she left it. The day she went to the hospital, she had a cup of crushed ice in one hand and the towel in the other. After Dan was born Ma was busy with the baby and my duties really intensified. It was summer vacation from school, but not from the restaurant.

My father had a bad trait. He didn't like to part with his money, even to pay his bills. He would come up with any excuse to get out of paying bills. The owner of the building had a soda company also on the north side, and he supplied us with some soda products. Now dad was not paying the rent regularly and not paying for the soda either. One day a kid bought an orange soda, and it had a small mouse in it. It was a very small mouse. My father was out-raged. He called the owner and said he wanted to see him right away. When the owner of the building arrived, an argument ensued. My father said he would sue him for every penny he had. The owner said he would make it right and knock off some of the money that my father owed him. My father laughed and told him he would never get a penny from him. The same thing was happening with the meat market. Our tab ran into the hundreds of dollars, and my father would put off paying the bill. Finally the butcher would not give us credit. I would have to bring the money and buy three pounds at a time; that was the max the butcher would sell us at one time. This was very stressful for me! I would have to run to the meat market two or three times a day sometimes. We also bought meat at other places. But by now the word was out that we had to pay cash.

Paying cash should have not been a problem, in fact, even with six kids we were taking in a lot of money. Some nights on the weekend I counted as much as seven hundred dollars. But where was it all going? I never knew, and I never found out. My father was the poorest money manager I ever heard of, even to this day. I was thirteen years old near the end of the restaurant run. I came up with two ideas that were earning money. First on a Friday and Saturday night, I roped off the back room and charged twenty-five cents to go into the dance floor. The teenagers came by the hundreds. There was this one kid who would put on a show with a broom. He would play an Elvis song on the Jukebox, and use the broom like a guitar. He was hilarious! Even when the high schoolers had a school dance, they all ended up at Lucky's. The second thing I came up with was the one dollar pizza. It was a nine inch pizza I baked in a small electric oven. While shopping one day, I came across these pizza shells in the bakery. I begged my father to buy some, which he did to my surprise. We had this little oven that just held the shell. We already had the sauce cooked up, so all I needed was some peppers and pepperoni. I sold a lot of the pizzas, and my father was surprised at it and let me sell them as long as he got the money. I never got paid anything, nor did I expect anything. "You are eating and sleeping, what more do you want?" my father would say. By the end of the following school year we were forced to move. I was in the end of my seventh school year with only a month to go till summer.

Raising Chickens

Our move was out of town, first to Mexico for a while, then up on route eleven in the town of Pulaski. I got enrolled in school just in time for final test. I did okay and was moved into the eighth grade. Some of my siblings did not fare as well and had to repeat the grade. The Pulaski home was an old farm house. There was a lot of land around the house, and my father decided to do some farming. It lasted about one day. He started to plow with an old cleat tractor, pulling a set of plows that were designed for horses. I sat on the plows, and he pulled it along. When he turned around, the plows would flip over and I would be thrown off. We dug up the backyard with these deep furrows but couldn't figure how to smooth the ground out. Dad said we'd finish it the next day. We never went back there again.

We did start getting chickens and ducks. We used the same ploy we used when we lived on Dingle Hole Road. When you buy chicken feed, the farm store would give you baby chicks. We got an incubator and raised chickens. Meantime, my father did some mechanical work. Paul and I did a lot of this with him. My work went from frying meat to removing engine parts almost over night. We had this cleat track tractor, which resembled a bulldozer. It started with a crank. My father took the engine out and put a Chevy six in it. We used it that winter to push the snow. Paul and I would take engines out and do all sorts of mechanical work; I had grease on my hands and arms most of the time. After a while we had a lot of chickens. It was our main source of food: eggs and chickens. Dad eked out a meager living with just getting by repairing a car or welding something for somebody.

All of us kids got the mumps while we lived there. It was a painful experience. I remember my mother making donuts and sprinkling powdered sugar on them, and we were so sick and our mouths so sore we couldn't eat them. A visiting nurse gave us some comfort in medicine form, and after about two weeks we recovered.

We didn't have an inside toilet there. It was out back off the kitchen door about thirty feet. We used a phone book for toilet paper. The shed was a three seater, although I can't really remember anyone sharing the shed. The door on the outhouse was a board with a spring attached to the inside. The spring held the door closed. There was no latch on the door, so we would stick a piece of paper from the phone book in the door to indicate it was occupied. We had a big barrel out behind the shed to burn our trash. When it got full we dumped it over and kept burning. As a result, the backyard had a lot of ash and partially burned papers. Of course the wind helped to move the trash further back into the woods area. Winter was tough, and it reminded me of Dingle Hole Road.

The Packard Hearse

One day my father found out about an old car he might be able to pick up in Pulaski. So we took a ride up, and my cousin Bob was with us. He had been living in his car in our driveway for a while. The car we went to see belonged to the undertaker in Pulaski. He had this old hearse in a shed for a couple of years and had no luck in selling it. The small barn

sat down grade from the road about fifty feet. The under-
taker and my father were talking in the driveway about the
terms of the deal. Bob and I went down and swung open
the doors on the barn. The car was tucked in with almost
no room to get behind it. It was a '48 Packard hearse, jet
black, with a beautiful chrome grill. The hood had a flying
lady ornament. There were spares mounted on the fenders
in black covers. Mounted on the covers were fancy chrome
mirrors. The car was covered in dust. My father backed
his car to the Packard and chained on to it. He pulled and
pulled, but the big old car would only rock slightly. He got
out and motioned to Bob and me to get behind and push.
We worked ourselves around in back of the old funeral
car. Bob, who always wore a white T-shirt, was trying to
keep him-self away from the dusty car, but his T-shirt was
black by the time we got to the back of the car. We started
to push, Bob leaned into the car and grunted with a hefty
push, but the car wouldn't budge. My father got out of the
family car and came to the front of the hearse and asked
us if we were pushing. Bob again grabbed the rear bumper
and wedged himself against the barn back. He told me to
push, and together we pushed with all our might. This time
the car moved about three inches. Bob was cursing the car
and the barn and everything in between. He leaned into
the back window and asked what was in this thing as he
attempted to wipe the dust off the back window. He cupped
his face with his hands and peered into the back window.
Suddenly he bolted over the car and down the road. My
father was chasing him as he was running off. I could hear
them off in the distance but could not make out what they
were saying. I looked into the back of the car. There was a
long wicker casket lying in the back of the hearse. Bob was
apparently frightened by the casket. I was a little amused
by this revelation because Bob was a big man who seemed

fearful of nothing. They were out in the street arguing. Bob said he wasn't going near the car, and my father was telling him to get down there and push that car. It was no use; Bob was not going near the car. I crawled back out, and the undertaker was coming out of the house. He must have heard the commotion between my father and Bob. He went to the car and told me to crawl into the driver's seat and take the car out of gear, which I did. Then he motioned to my father to get in his car and pull the car out. Out it came with no trouble. He pulled me and the car up on the road and stopped. He and Bob argued a little about Bob steering the car back to the house while the undertaker was removing the wicker casket. When Bob saw the casket, he got into my father's car on the passenger side and told my father not to talk to him. Bob was noticeably frightened. I ended up steering the car back, and Bob never looked back even once to see the hearse behind him.

With this new information about Bob's fear of the car, I had a plan to play a trick on him when we got back at the house. Now Bob was sleeping in his car at night in our driveway. That night he put his seats down; he had one of those cars where the seats reclined into a bed, and he retired. Paul and I watched from the window. Early the next morning Paul and I went outside and pushed the Packard up next to his car. Bob would sleep till noon if you let him. But Paul and I were calling him from the window.

"Bob, wake up, Bob, wake up."

He looked up at us and wiped his eyes and asked what time it was. We excitedly pointed to the Packard parked next to his car; he looked slowly around then jumped out of his car. He ran down the driveway. Before he realized where he was, he began to call my father. We got hollered at from both men. My dad was mad because he was woken up at the ungodly hour of nine o'clock in the morning.

Bob grabbed me by the neck and squeezed me a little, and through his teeth he told me to move the car or he would move my neck off my shoulder. We moved the car, but we always joked with him about the Packard.

We had a lot of fun with the old hearse. When our parents took us along shopping we would stay in the car. One of us would lie in the back under a sheet while the rest of us sat in the front seat pretending to be crying. When someone approached us, we would point to the back and say, "Our brother, our brother." When the person looked in the back, the one under the sheet would sit up. One lady screamed and ran away, and another time a young man jumped back with a jerk. When he figured he'd been fooled, he hollered at us for almost giving him a heart attack. Our parents never knew about our antics. When they came back to the car we would be giggling, and they would wonder what we were laughing about.

We eventually stripped out all the funeral stuff out of the Packard, like the rollers and flower cages near the back windows. The car weighed 6000 pounds and had a straight eight engine with a three speed standard transmission. When it was empty it had almost no power, but loaded with the family and other things, it barely moved under its own power. Once you got it going it was okay. We also had a 1953 Studebaker pickup truck. It ran well, but we had a time getting all the family in it to go somewhere.

Paul and I went outside and pushed the Packard up next to Bob's car.

How I Met the KKK

ONE DAY MY PARENTS AND I WERE RIDING IN THE Studebaker, going into town. Dad started talking to Ma about a secret they had and wanted to share it with me. They hemmed and hawed for a few minutes, then my dad proudly asked what I thought about moving away from New York.

"Why," I asked.

It is this next few years that became the most confusing to my memory. I remember starting out for Florida with the old Packard. We had a big auction sale a few days before we left and raised a few dollars selling all our furniture and tools and chickens. My Aunt Millie got a lot of the chickens. We delivered them to her home in Fairmount in crates. Her husband, Uncle Tony, was furious. She had to kill and dress over a hundred chickens.

The trip was a disaster from the start when we hit Pennsylvania, because the car could not make the hills. There was no super highway then, just a regular road with two-way traffic. We were stuck on the side of the road halfway up the hill. We got a gas station mechanic to pull us up the hill with his four-wheel drive Jeep. The Jeep was spinning its wheels all the way up the hill, and it cost my father five dollars. Down the hill we went, and half way up the next hill we were stopped again. The car just had no power to pull all the things we had in the car. So he called the gas station again. After a while the mechanic came rolling up in his Jeep again. He seemed a little angry, and he was hollering at my father about the car being too heavy. He agreed to do one more pull, and that was it. In all we got a few people to help us over the mountains in Pennsylvania. When we got into the lower states the roads were flatter and although the trip was long and slow we finally made it to our destination which was Jacksonville Florida.

I attended three schools in Florida, all in the Jacksonville area. On the first day of school I had a test on the thirteen colonies. I had no trouble and got a high score. The teacher was amazed. I found the school a little behind, because they were covering things I had studied a year before in New York. I was ahead of them in every subject. Regina, who had struggled in some areas, was coasting. The big problem was the culture shock we got from the people living there. In 1958, they were still fighting the civil war. We were the enemies. For the first time in my life I was called a Yankee. At first I thought of the baseball team, and then it became apparent that we were not wanted there.

We moved from one place to another in a short time and ended up renting a restaurant on the main drag in Jacksonville. We lived in a small apartment attached to the rear of the restaurant. Dad was in town setting some things up when we got a knock on the door. My mother answered it to find a short, stocky man standing on the door mat. He informed my mother that we would have to move back to New York, or she would find her husband floating in the Jacksonville river. We later learned he was the grand wizard of the Jacksonville klu klux klan. When My father returned, my mother and us kids were huddled in the back room with the lights off.

Dad's was determined to stay! We opened the restaurant, and it did okay for a while. I even set up my pizza oven and was selling pizzas for 99 cents a piece for a nine incher. We found the laws a little strange there. This was the first time I attended a segregated school. All public bathrooms were for white people, unless it said colored. This also applied to drinking fountains. It was strange to go to a set of drinking fountains and see signs on some of them marked for colored. If a colored person ever drank from a white fountain, they would be jailed or beaten on the spot. I frankly was bewildered and frightened by the whole thing. I just couldn't figure out why a colored person had to drink from a different fountain. The worst thing for me was the attitude of the kids in school. They would ask me if I hated colored people, but they never used the word *colored*. I would tell them I hate no one, and ask them why I should hate them. Then they would holler to each other, and point at me here's "*N*" lover. I became the instant enemy of the school crowd. There were a few that were not vocal, but not many. My parents never used that kind of language, and would not allow it. My brothers and sisters never swore or used profanity, neither did I. In fact the kids in the Jacksonville school were very polite, with yes sir, and no ma'am, but they swore like sailors.

Paul and I had a lot of fights in school because we were Yankees. In one school when the gym coach found out I was from Syracuse, he took me in his office and shut the door. That year the Syracuse football team was number one in the nation. They had a powerful team. The coach wanted me to reveal the secret behind the power of the Syracuse team.

"What do they have?" he asked. I didn't know what to tell him, but I remembered when I was in the Syracuse schools reading about how the coach would get the boys up early and have them run, then they all sat down to an egg and steak breakfast. So I told the coach that, then added, "And you know down here they eat grits for breakfast." It was a major mistake in my deployment of my explanation.

He got red and said something about grits being a southern staple. He took me out and introduced me to the boys in gym class. Then told them that I was from Syracuse, where the men are stronger than the Jacksonville men. He further tried to press the point by making me wrestle every boy in class for the duration of my stay there. I held my own even when the coach would deliberately leave the gym so the boys could fight with me.

After a while, the Klu Klux Klan began to put more pressure on us to leave. Dad started a private detective agency and had a badge and gun. He called his nephews and asked them to come down. Now my father had, in essence, his own police department. My cousins had guns and badges and patrolled to protect businesses in the area. There was a show down at a truck stop one night, and after that the men from the Klan eased up on us. Their plan was to get us out with a legal move to outlaw the business my father had. After a legal struggle, my father relented and made plans to leave the state. We closed the restaurant, which by now was not doing any business because of the boycott from the klan.

Out of Florida

W<small>E MOVED INTO A CEMENT BLOCK HOUSE, PARTIALLY</small> finished, in a nice neighborhood west of Jacksonville. It was 1959 in the spring of the year. I was collecting newspapers and selling them. I was making about ten dollars a week. I had the papers stacked in a small shed on the property. One day I opened the shed door and setting on the pile of papers was a large snake. I shut the door and never opened it again. I was forced out of the paper business by a snake. Sue Ellen was born at that time, and that rounded off the family with eight kids. My cousin John Fortino and Bob left first; Tom remained till we were ready to go. Dad was building a trailer to haul the junk he had accumulated. The trailer was about twenty feet long, and he built walls and a roof on it. It was a heavy house trailer. He piled things to the ceiling, old motors, lamps, books, and clothes. The car he had was an old 1951 Hudson and had no trailer hitch on it. Plus the Hudson had no power; it burned a lot of oil. He had swapped the Hudson for a 52 caddy we had but would need a better car for the trip.

He came home with another car, a Nash Rambler American. The car was a station wagon. He ordered us to get in the back behind the seat. Regina, Paul, and I got in and were pressed against the back window. He hollered at us to get away from the window, but we couldn't. There was no way to put ten people in that car. Not to mention we

would have to put food and clothes in the car also. To add
to his dilemma, he put the trailer on the car, and the back
bumper went right into the ground.

"Wow, I think the car will get to New York before
us," I said.

"Keep it up," he replied. "You are asking for it. I chuck-
led to myself, but I knew we would never go in that car. I
couldn't figure out why he couldn't see that. He unhooked
the car and left. He was gone for about three hours, and
when he returned, he had a 51 Chevy suburban, plenty big
enough to do the job. I never learned where he got it or how
he got it.

DAD WAS A WHEELER DEALER. He would trade or swap on a
whim. One time we were driving down the road in Florida.
When I say we, I mean all of us, my mother, brothers, and
sisters. Dad was driving our big, long green Fleetwood '52
Cadillac. As we were going along the road, dad noticed a
car facing the other way off to the side of the road with the
hood up. The driver was standing in front of the car peering
under the hood into the engine compartment. Dad went
by and looked back in his mirror. Then he made a quick
U-turn and pulled up behind the stalled car. He got out
and walked up to the front of the car and began to speak to
the driver. We watched as they both leaned over the fender
into the car's front compartment. After a few minutes my
father shut the hood, and the two kept talking in front of
the other car. It wasn't twenty minutes from the time we
stopped till dad came walking back to our car. He came
around to the passenger side and opened the front door.

"Get out," he said, "and take all our things out too." He
had just swapped cars. The other car was a cool '51 Hudson

Hornet, the dash was wood, and the radio played. Down there you could do that because the plates stayed with the car. In a short time we were driving away with the Hudson. It had its problems, but it ran okay. I guess it needed a fuel pump. Dad figured it out and thought it was worth the swap.

WELL, WE HAD THE CHEVY SUBURBAN, and it was a truck that could do the job of pulling the huge trailer. So we loaded up and started back to New York. Tom and Joan Fortino left with us; they had a big Packard sedan and pulled a small utility trailer. The Chevy Suburban was loaded to the hilt. The family just sort of sat on the top of everything on the seats.

My cousin Tom would not drive the slow speed we were traveling. He would drive sixty and wait in a gas station for us up the road. His car had a bad transmission, but Tom didn't care. My father would tell him to go easy.

Tom would say, "I'll go easy all right; I'll go an easy sixty."

We did all right from Jacksonville to the Florida border then the wheel broke off our trailer. A Georgian farmer bought the trailer, and now that Chevy Suburban was really loaded. We had a pile on top about five feet high. The inside was so full; we were crawling against the ceiling. Dad also got Tom and Joan to put some things in their trailer. Joan was furious and was hollering at Tom in the car. We could see her arms waving frantically in the air. Tom just shrugged his shoulders and kept driving.

It was a slow trip; my father drove about thirty-five miles per hour. He was in no hurry. I think he never was a fast driver. He did drive fast on a few occasions, but generally, thirty-five or forty was his speed. We got into Virginia, and Tom's car really started to act up. He was barely making the hills. The car had a bad smell, and my father said his transmission was going. Sure enough it broke down on the side of the road on a long hill in Maryland. Tom called his brothers, and Ronald and John and their grandfather came from New York. We were waiting for about a day before help arrived. Ronald hooked on to the big Packard, with the trailer, and pulled it back to New York. We followed them back but could not keep up. Even with the heavy load, John wanted to drive as fast as he could go. We plodded behind, not getting into the city for hours after Tom got back.

THE FLORIDA TRIP WAS LIKE A NIGHTMARE. The things that we encountered while in Florida were almost unbelievable. The Southern people at the time were very indignant about having Northern people coming down to live there. What my family and I did not realize was that there were people coming to the south for the specific purpose of fighting a battle over civil discrepancies between the blacks and whites. The world down there was different than in the north. Blacks had no rights and were treated as second class citizens. They could not sit at a lunch counter where whites sat, and there was usually an area set aside with a table or a few booths with a sign hanging which read, "Colored." They could not drink from the same fountain nor use the same toilet. Well, I remember stopping in a gas station and having to use the toilet around the back of the garage. There were three small rooms: men, women, and "colored." The toilet for the "colored" people had no door, and the room was littered with trash. The toilet itself could be seen as I passed the spot. There was no toilet seat, and the toilet was absolutely filthy. It touched me so that to this day I have that scene indelibly imprinted into my mind.

There was an atmosphere of war there in 1958. Not a war against an invading alien army, but a war against citizens of our own land. There were laws against blacks that applied only to them. Those laws were viscously applied and carried out. If a black person was beaten, it was assumed he or she deserved it. The "colored" people were fearful of whites because their families would be punished regardless of who in the black community broke one of the black laws.

Our parents never taught us to discriminate against other races. My father would say we should leave them alone and mind our own business. He was not a crusader for civil rights; I don't think he saw the whole war thing going on. Neither did I or my brothers or sisters. We were actually taken back by the discrimination against the blacks. In school the kids would question us on our side in the issue, which was no issue to us. We were having enough trouble just surviving. We were called Yankees, which I first thought of it as being from New York. But after a while it became clear that these people hated us.

Eventually they starved us out. They isolated us and would not let us find a way to earn a living there. Later I would remember the first experience in the south and be amazed at how united they were in their losing effort to drive the desegregation movement from their states. Once the word got out that we were from New York, we had trouble even buying groceries from the local market. We would buy a fifty pound bag of potatoes from a farmers market by sending someone they did not suspect as being from us. We would feast on the potatoes and try to figure out how to get our next meal in the meantime. There were days when we did not eat anything. There were days when we managed to get a box of oatmeal, and it would suffice the family for the day. My mother would cook the oatmeal and give it to us around noon, figuring to split up the day so we would not be too hungry at night. We would go to school with no food, and many days would endure the day with no food. I knew what it was like to go a couple days at a time without eating.

Finally my father decided to leave; I think he held out for a while because of two points: the first being he did not accept or understand the whole civil rights war going on at the time. He knew that blacks were being mistreated in Florida, and the whites there hated blacks, but he did not understand the full scope of the problem. Secondly, he was stubborn. He thought he would overcome their bigotry and win their approval. He refused to hear our pleas to leave the south. Maybe it would be a defeat to his ego that he made the wrong decision to go there in the first place. It was a happy day when we finally heard we were leaving.

Restarting in New York

With that finally behind us, I found myself back in a country setting in upstate New York. We lived for a while in a house deep in the woods on a country dirt road. The old house was in poor shape, and I think my father made a deal with the owner to make repairs in exchange for rent. There was no toilet in the house, and there was no toilet outside either. We would go into the woods to do our duties with a small shovel. After a while we had an area back there quite large. The whole thing was terrible, but we learned how to live in the raw.

This old house held a treasure in the attic. There were about fifty large pictures in beautiful, curved glass frames. There were pictures of some family and some paintings also. When our cousin Bob saw them, he told us to take the backs off because sometimes people put money or other treasures back behind the pictures. Regina and I tore all the frame backs off; we found nothing. When my father found out what we did, he thought we were crazy and hollered at Bob because he thought we might have gotten cut on the glass. The irony of the whole thing was that the frames and glass themselves were probably worth thousands of dollars, but we were too ignorant to realize it. When we left the house, we left all the frames and glass there in the attic. We heard that the house burned to the ground shortly after we moved when struck by lightening.

In the summer of that year we picked cherries on a farm, the whole family went out to the farm, including Bobby, our cousin. Bob didn't pick except to taste the cherries. He would set under a cherry tree with my father's guitar and play while we worked. Bobby was like my father, in that he liked to live by the deal rather than by actually working. The farmer had about a hundred acres of cherries. There were very large trees over twenty feet tall and new trees just six or eight feet tall. We only picked for about three or four weeks in all but made a pretty good income because we pooled all our cherries into one pot. I think I had the record in picking cherries. The farmer put me on the small trees one day and I went crazy. I picked twenty-three crates, at three cents a pound. My father liked the large trees; he would set up in the tree and whistle and sing. Bob would play and dad would sing or do his bird impressions. Near the end of our picking cherries, another farmer came by and wanted to borrow some workers to top onions. Guess who my father volunteered to go? I topped onions a few days with Mexican workers; we got along great. They taught me how to do it without cutting my hands all up. We worked as a team and got about five acres of onions out of the field.

Wolcott, New York

By this time we had made at least three moves and were living in Sayer, New York. I started school, but after a month we moved to Wolcott, New York, where I was in the ninth grade. We lived just outside Wolcott in an old farm house with a barn across the street. It was one of the first places I lived where I had a neighbor friend my age that came over to play. We would play chess. We didn't have actual chess men, so we used sea shells. We had differently shaped shells; one for the pawns and rooks, and etc. We had to color one set to tell whose were whose. My friend's name was Gary, and he had a sister named Helen. Helen was Regina's age, and they were good friends also. Helen had sharp blue eyes and was pretty. I had to keep telling Regina to take her friend to another room and leave us alone, because Helen would tease me constantly. Gary and Helen lived with their parents and grandfather in the house next door about one hundred yards from our place.

After a few months my father got into trouble with the law, and he fled the state, leaving my mother with us eight kids. We did not know where he went for a while, but got word he was living in Pennsylvania. We continued to live there till after Christmas of 1959. I became good friends with Gary, and sometimes we would play chess all night on a weekend. I was doing well in school and liked history and math. My spelling was still poor but passing. Regina was a good speller and would never let me forget it. She also had a wicked temper like Paul, and one day stabbed me in the back with a pencil. Another time she stuck a pencil in my cheek, where I still have the scar to this day. I never participated in any school activities as I was very shy and stayed home all the time. We rode the bus to school; the Wolcott school was just outside of the town, and we lived away from the town. So I never actually went into the town of Wolcott to do any shopping or anything. I know I attended the high school, but if someone asked me how big the town was, I had no idea.

I was a naïve fifteen-year-old boy, and up to this point had never had a girlfriend. In fact, I never had a girl friend till I was in the twelfth grade, when I met little Franny Jo Parker. But the next experience I had would be like a shock to my system. My aunt Millie and uncle Frank came to visit us in Wolcott to bring a message from my father. He had a job in Philadelphia and wanted us to go there to live with him. My mother resisted at first, but then relented when urged by my father's family. My mother could never say no, (she had eight kids) her temperament was submissive and could not carry on a conversation with out crying. So she said okay, so we left the small hamlet of Wolcott with it's country roads, farms, and straightlaced school. I had no idea how laid back it was till I entered the school system in Philadelphia, Pennsylvania.

The Philly Civil Rights Movement

We arrived in Philly in mid-winter sometime after Christmas. My father had an upstairs apartment located on 53rd street. It was a modest apartment with three small bedrooms. He had been working in a garage as a mechanic. The year was 1959, and the city was in the midst of the civil rights movement in America. I was unaware of the conflicts. As I said earlier, we did not have a problem with the color of a man's skin, and my main problem was survival. Bobby was with us again. He had come down before us and was living with my father before we arrived. Bob didn't work. I don't mean he was broken; he just didn't have steady employment. Bob lived by dealing and swapping things and living here and there. It was the life he chose, and we never questioned him or harassed him about it. He never stayed in one place very long, as people were always looking for him. You could say he was popular. When we lived in Florida, Bob borrowed a car and drove back to Syracuse. There were some people in Florida looking for their car, and I guess Bob had junked it.

After a few days, Regina and I walked down to the junior high school about eight blocks from our apartment. It was in the middle of the morning and the classes were in progress. We were greeted in the hall by a stout gentleman in a suit who asked us where we were going and why we were not in a class. We explained that we were new to the school and had not yet enrolled. He led us to the offices, and on the way gave us the riot act on conduct and procedures. It turns out the man was one of the school detectives hired by the city to patrol the school. We learned later that Regina and I were two of only a few white kids in the school. In fact, the school was made up of 98% African American children. A lot of the teachers and administrators were white. The office people processed our enrollment, and Regina and I were separated, with different teachers taking us around to the classes and introducing us to the teachers. When that was finished, we were told to go home and start fresh in the morning. With our maps of the school and our schedules in place, we left the building. The school detective followed us to the door and admonished us to go straight home.

The City of Philadelphia was a busy place, not at all like the sleepy little town we had just left. The police had bright red cars and seemed to be everywhere. From the school to 53rd street was a straight shot. We had only one corner to turn, and our apartment was in the middle of the block. On the corner was the five and dime store, as we passed it we didn't notice exactly what was going on at first, just a commotion, with people hollering and carrying signs. I don't think we even mentioned it to our parents when we got back to the apartment. The younger kids were enrolled in a grade school in the other direction. Ma had taken them, and that's why us older kids had to go alone to enroll.

The next day we rose early and started off to school with the brown bag lunches my mother had prepared. As we approached the corner store, the commotion was still going on. There were cameras from the television stations, there were men holding microphones, and a crowd of about thirty or forty people surrounding the corner, and there were police cars everywhere. We worked our way around the corner, this time observing closer the commotion. It was some type of protest. African American people and some whites were holding signs; they walked in a big circle chanting something about counter seats and the right to sit with whites. It turns out, this demonstration was one of the many in the nation over the rights of blacks to sit at the food counter with whites. We only stayed in Philly for a few months, but the demonstrations at that corner went on all the time we lived there. Later in life I saw a program on TV called *Eyes on the Prize,* in which that corner store was shown. I bet there is film somewhere showing Regina and I walking around the crowds. The cameras were there every morning and all day long. We were oblivious to that issue. We had no background or problems in that area in New York. Our short stay in Florida should have given us a clue, but we seemed to not see the great conflict yet. So on we went to our first day at the new school.

Junior High.

The school was called Sayer Junior High. As we approached the school, there were crowds of students gathered around the outside of the doors. We walked past them and found the school doors locked; the crowds laughed at us and mocked us. A boy approached me and struck up a conversation. He asked if we were new to the school, to which I replied it was our first day. He put his arm around me and led me away from Regina a few feet, and in a low tone began to point to a girl sitting on the side of the steps of the school. He kept asking me something about the girl, but I couldn't make him out. Then he asked in a louder voice if I wanted her. *Wanted her?* I thought. "Why would I want her?" I replied to the boy. I kept looking over to Regina to see if she was okay. The events that happened to me there in the next few weeks and months were like a nightmare. I had never encountered the things that I saw going on at that school anywhere in my past, and I would never see in any school the things I saw there.

On the first day of school I was propositioned to pay for sex with a girl in the schoolyard. In homeroom, boys tried to sell me marijuana for smoking. On my way to my first class, I was grabbed by three large boys and dragged into the men's room and mugged. When I came out of the mens room, I was dazed, and my clothes were ripped and torn; my shirt was pulled out of my pants. I had gone only a few feet when I felt the big hand on the back of my neck. It was the school detective. He began to rebuke me for having my shirt out of my pants. I tried to tell him I was assaulted, but he wouldn't hear it. Squeezing now even more tightly, he warned me to keep my problems to myself and tuck in the shirt. He squeezed harder. "Tuck it in," he said between his teeth. I began to tuck my shirt in as he asked. "Ah, better," he said. "Now get to your next class and stay out of trouble." Where was I? What was this place? I thought that was bad, but before long I learned it was the tip of the iceberg. I had never seen such a lack of morals by students or teachers and staff than at that school.

The lunch room was a very large room with tables in the center. Located on one side was two booths completely closed except for the window in the front with bars on it. It was very much like ticket booths you would see at a fair or in front of a movie theater. They were there to make change for the meals. All meals were paid for with exact change. The other side of the lunch room had a glass wall. Behind it, the food was served through a thin slot in the glass. There were coin slots at each opening, and the students would put the coins into the slot, the money would run down a glass tray into a glass box. The server would count the money and slide the food through the slot to the student. Whether the purchase was for a dish of potatoes or a slice of cake, everybody bought the meal through the glass. I got the impression the school had some problems in the past with keeping the students from stealing food. The school detectives were stationed in the lunch room and stood with their arms folded, watching the students just like in the movies. When I walked into the cafeteria, one of the school detectives told me to sit down and eat and not dilly dally. I sat at a table alone but was quickly surrounded by some of the kids in some of my classes. Then, without warning, one grabbed me from behind in a headlock choke hold, while others wrestled the lunch bag from my hands. I looked out of the corner of my eye to see the detective look at my dilemma then quickly turn his head in another direction. It happened very fast, the perpetrators were running out the side door gobbling my sandwich as they ran. I called to the detective and began to tell him what happened; he raised his hand out in front of me and stopped me. He reminded me to eat quickly next time. I sat back down, and a few others came and sat near me. One boy had bought a piece of cake. As soon as he got it through the glass slot he spit on it. Even as he came to the table he continued to spit on the cake. This was meant to ward off any would-be thieves who might think to take his meal. I saw this replayed by most of the students during my stay there in that school. I went without food the first day. I had been robbed earlier and didn't have even a nickel to buy a bag of chips.

One of my classes was American History. Although, I don't think we studied much history in that class. The teacher was an Italian man formerly from New York City. Every day the same routine took place in his class. After a quick roll call, he called on one of the girls to come up and watch the class while he ran some errands. The girl would then let some of the boys take some of the girls back in the closet for a little promiscuity. Sometimes the teacher would return before everyone was finished and would dismiss himself again till after the bell. There was a lot of that misbehavior in most of the classes. The art class was another place where art was brought to a new form. The teacher would charge the boys for sex in the closet of the room every day. The rest of us would set at a single large table and doodle on a piece of paper till the end of class. Sometimes two or three boys took turns in the closet each day. At the end of class she would collect the doodles and mark them. I never saw my doodles or marks, but was told they would determine my grade.

The hardest class was mechanical drawing class. The teacher was an elderly black man who was about six foot three and had to weigh 275 pounds. All his lessons were centered in the discussion of the superiority of the black man; what the black man did for America, how the black man was oppressed and held down by whites and etc. I was the only white kid in the class. About the second week he called me up to the front of the class and said he wanted to prove his point. He picked a boy who was about my size and ordered us to sit at the table in the front and have an arm wrestling match. I made a big mistake; I put the kids arm down with no effort. I was a wiry kid and arm wrestling was something I did well. Back in the restaurant I would arm wrestle kids two or three years older than me and never lost. This teacher was noticeably upset and picked out another to arm wrestle me. This went on every day with me arm wrestling one or two boys each class. Thinking back on the whole thing, I could have saved myself a lot of headaches if

I just let one of them beat me. I guess a little of my Italian ego would not allow me to just lie down.

All the boys there thought they were Joe Louis. The gym class was a giant class of sixty-five or seventy boys. The coach was a tall, lanky black man who demanded submission and respect from the class. He commanded his whistle like a traffic cop. The slightest infraction would send him into a rage, and he would whip that person with the long strap of boondoggle fastened to his whistle. The gym floor had little white balls painted into rows with a bold black number in each ball. Every boy had a number given to them, and when the coach blew his whistle, you were to go to your number and sit on the floor. At the end of the class he would dismiss each row slowly to give everybody a chance to go downstairs to the locker room without stampeding each other. Most of the time our gym class was spent playing basketball. The walls were lined with basket hoops, and it was possible to play twenty half court games at one time.

I met one boy there who was Japanese. He would steal a car almost every day. One day I saw him drive up in a new Chevy. He parked the car along the side of the playground next to the steel, chain link fence. We were in the homeroom at the start of the day when another boy called him to the window telling him to come and see his new car being towed by the police. He would shake his head and say, "I'll have another one by tomorrow morning." And he usually did.

The homeroom class was something else. They had a party every Friday night. The class would collect two dollars from each person and with it rent a motel room for Friday night. I never participated in their debauchery, but every Monday they would talk about the party to each other and go on about who did what or so on. It was a constant barrage of filthy language and conversation. One day into my third week, a girl passed out in one of my classes. She was brought to the infirmary where she gave birth to a baby boy. We were in the ninth grade. After that in a few days, the city made the school examine all the girls in junior and senior school in Philadelphia. In our school alone the paper reported that 35 percent of the girls were pregnant. I was not surprised, but no changes were made there except the report was given to parents.

When we left the school, we were escorted along the way to the apartment by a steady stream of police cars. As we approached the corner, the crowds intensified. The police would emerge from their cruisers with night sticks and prevent people from gathering on corners. I often saw young men beaten and arrested because they refused to keep moving along the sidewalk. Regina and I were fearful of the walk home and would talk about what happened that day to mom. After school we never left the apartment once we got home. Each day we would try to prepare for the school day by rehearsing what we would do or say in certain situations. Going to school in the past had its worries, like when I had to take a test, but this was a different type of test; a test of survival.

There were many fights in the school, almost all involved knives. All the people carried knives, including the girls. One day two girls were fighting in the hall, I came around the corner right in the middle of the fight. A short girl was swinging a knife at another girl and pushed her against a board and stuck her in the arm. I sure didn't want that girl mad at me. Teachers were reluctant to intervene, and when they did they often were injured themselves. The school detectives were mysteriously missing during these fights and only emerged after the fight had quelled. I think the teachers were just as fearful as Regina and I and some carried knives and would let it be known.

Hospital Time

My tenure at the Philly school ended abruptly one day after gym class when I was attacked by almost the whole body of the class. One boy attacked me during the class and the coach saw it. He screamed at the boy and began to whip him with the boondoggle cord. Some of the other boys began to point to me and say, "You are dead, you are dead." The coach blew his whistle, and we all retreated to our spot on the gym floor. I was in the second row, and when I got to the lockers, the boys began to crowd around me. I kept saying I don't want any trouble, but it was drowned out by a roar of the crowd. I remember feeling a pain in my side and passing out. When I awoke, I was on the floor and a sneaker was coming towards my face and going out away. I felt no pain. The next thing I knew I was doused in water, and the coach was holding me up in his arms. They took me to the nurses' station on a stretcher. I laid in the infirmary for about two hours before taking me to the hospital. I was covered in human spit. My eyes were completely closed. I had welts and bruises all over my body. Fortunate for me we were in gym class, and the boys had gym clothes and not street clothes, or else they would have had their knives, and I would have been dead. After that, I never returned to the school.

The next day, two city detectives (who were black) came up to the apartment, knocking on the door. They wanted to interrogate me about the fight. My father refused to let them in the apartment, and instead brought me out in the upstairs hall. The policemen spoke to me at the top of the stairs. They asked me what happened and then asked if this was the first time I had been in trouble. That was the last straw for my father; he kicked one of cops down the stairs and hit the other. They went rolling down the stairs. He grabbed me and ran down the stairs, kicking past the police who were still falling. If it happened today, my father would have been arrested for a hate crime, just for the language he was using. We beat the cops to the car and sped off to the police station. At the station, my father carried me in and sat me on a bench in the main hall. My eyes were so swollen I could only see out of one eye and not very well. I was unable to walk, my father carried me on his shoulder. My legs were all purple from the kicking I received. A sergeant was seated behind a tall desk, and my father began to berate him about sending black police to the house to investigate the beating of his son. He had a striped tee shirt and dungarees and looked like Popeye. While he was hollering, the two detectives came in from the side. He pointed in their direction and started for them. All of a sudden the whole police force seemed to appear. There were about seven or eight police who dove at my father. The wrestling lasted a few minutes, and dad came up with handcuffs screaming the same obscenities about the black officers. The captain of the precinct appeared and held out his hands towards my father, trying to calm him down. The other officers were still holding him. Finally, the captain ordered him to be put in a room nearby, and the captain came over to me and carried me in the room also, as I could not walk straight or hold myself up very well. In the room were three or four policemen and the captain and my father and me. The captain was very apologetic and was able to calm my father, which surprised me. Then they told us about something that happened just that morning. One of the boys involved in beating me had stabbed and killed a white boy in front of his house. He explained that there was a war going on in the city between the blacks and whites. He had hoped by sending black police officers, we might have softened our feelings towards blacks. He realized he had made a mistake, but his words now were softening my father. He apologized for causing a ruckus but wanted to know what was going to be done about the problem. The policemen looked at each other and realized my father could not grasp the greatness of the struggle. We never hated the African Americans. My father thought of the problem as a local, isolated problem in the school, not as a civil problem between races.

From that moment my father decided to get out of Philadelphia. When we got back home, he informed my mother and the other kids that we were moving. We didn't know where, but we knew we were moving. My parents had been going to a church there in Philly, not regular church on a Sunday morning, but on a week night, and it was hopping. There were about one thousand people there on a Wednesday night, people from all denominational backgrounds. My father had gotten religion, and decided to go into the ministry. He had a background in the church; his mother was a devout Christian. Some of his brothers and sisters were Christians. His mother made him go to church when he was young, so he had some knowledge of the bible. Back when we lived on Dingle Hole Road he had brought us to church a few times, and I remembered it and thought it so out of place at the time. I remember showing up in church with our family; how everyone looked at us as if we were bald neck roosters.

Evangelistic Understudy

We lived there in Philly for a few weeks after my incident in the school. During that time I was unable to move around much. I was beginning to feel better, and the school truant officer came to the house and wanted to know how I was doing. He was lucky to get out without a physical confrontation with my father. He never came back. We packed up and moved down to Richmond Virginia. Somehow my father obtained ordination papers with some outfit in Pennsylvania. He bought a tent from the army and navy store and was set to start preaching.

I entered the school in Richmond as soon as we got there. Now about this school; it was totally segregated. Richmond had built three schools for the blacks and kept one in the inner city for whites. I don't know why, but the Richmond school was not at all like the Philly school. It was a bigger school, but the students were there to get an education. The military school R.O.T.C. was big on the campus. The students were so polite; it was like I landed on a different planet. They treated each other with an almost unbelievable courtesy. A lot of the boys had military dress, and if one had rank, he would be respected for his rank. It was unbelievable. After what I had just been through, I thought this must be like Heaven. I adjusted to the training in no time; I had not had any school training in Philly at all. I was able to bring my grades up, and by the end of the school year I had passing grades. This was only a short time because I was attacked on St. Patrick's day in March and had lost at least three weeks after that before enrolling in Richmond. I had trouble understanding the southern drawl. One time a teacher asked me to open a winder, and I just looked at her. She asked again, and I squinted at her with a look of confusion. The other kids giggled and couldn't figure out what my problem was. Finally she came over to me and pointed to the window and said, "Please open the winder." When I got home, I told my parents what happened, and my father showed up in the principal's office the next day to complain about the misuse of the language. My father loved the opportunity to argue like a lawyer. He produced a dictionary and asked the teacher to pronounce the word as it was written in the book. She peered at the book and said, "Winder." Then my father asked her to look at the book and see how the word was pronounced. She looked again down at the book, then across at the principal, then at me, and said, "Winder." I really thought my father was going to slap her. The principal told my father that they didn't need Yankees to come down to teach them how to talk. My father closed the book and said, "You are right; I'm sorry." Later he told me when the principal said, "Yankee," he remembered Florida, and said he was sorry. But under his breath he said, "For you." There was a lot of bigotry in Richmond; they were still fighting the civil war. Their history book on the war between the states ended with the statement, "The south shall rise again." However, I encountered very little animosity with any students over my being a "Yankee" at that school. I was not an advocate for the white; neither did I dislike the black people, even though both sides seemed to dislike me.

Another first was the smoking. Smoking was allowed on the first floor in the cafeteria and all halls. It was strange to see kids lighting up in the lunchroom, or in the hall on the way to class. Of course it smelled like an ashtray when you entered the school. I was offered a smoke every day but refused politely and never commented on their smoking. I figured it was their culture, and later on that year we would meet ministers from the Church of God who not only condoned smoking but smoked cigarettes and cigars themselves. The tobacco industry was powerful and supported the schools and the churches in Richmond.

The classes in the school were fairly easy. I found no taxing problems with the studies there, and at the end of the school year I was promoted to the tenth grade. As a matter of fact, I scored fairly high on final tests, which left some of the teachers surprised because of my lack of class-room participation. After all, the last time I had any actual studies was in Wolcott when I started the ninth grade. Children of my generation had a great advantage over the young people of today.

We didn't have the video games and other distractions of this age. While I could not study at home very well, I still could set and meditate on the things I learned in school. I had a tremendous memory and could focus on whole pages of a book. I could name just about every nation in the world by studying the world map for a while. In one of my lower grades I had a math teacher who taught us how to speed add and subtract. He could add columns of numbers quicker than a computer. I remembered some of his tactics later on to get through ninth grade math.

Another Hearse

My father had picked up another hearse during our stay in Richmond and painted his name on the side in big bold letters: *A.E. Luckette Evangelistic Assoc.* He would pick us up at school and sometimes would have to park in front of the school and wait for us. When school was over all the kids would pour out and stand around the car and gawk at it. He had a way of making a spectacle of himself. He had abandoned the clothes of the well-dressed Italian of Dingle Hole Road. His desires didn't change, they were just inconvenient. He still had his Stetson hat but hardly ever wore it.

My father had a small clothing store in Richmond. He collected used clothes and sold them at a cut rate price, much like the Salvation Army does today. I spent a lot of time during my school days in that store. When he picked me up after school we went there, and I kept the store while he went gallivanting around. He had some friends that owned a gas station. There were seven brothers, all big burly men. One day one of the younger brothers crashed his car and died in the accident. My father was called because he was a minister and this started a friendship that lasted for many years. Later in his life he went back to Richmond and renewed the friendship with the brothers.

Camping Out

When school was out, dad closed the store and we went camping. That's what I called it. It was the only way I could rationalize the situation. He had a rack on the top of the car which held the old army tent. The rack was once used by a group of singers called The Ozark Mountain Boys. He painted over their sign with green paint but the lettering still showed through. All our possessions were housed in the hearse. We started north and found a spot to park on the "Y" in the road. We pitched the tent and found a neighbor to supply electricity with an extension cord. Dad parked the car close to the road so the sign on his car could be seen by the passing cars. He visited a few churches and got some of the churches to come out and support his ministry. He would preach, sometimes to a small group of just a few folks, and called on me to pass the plate. One church, a Church of God, came out for a week but then abandoned us when the subject of smoking arose. The minister of that church, a heavy set older gentleman, smoked cigars through the service. When the service was over, we stacked the chairs and rolled out our bedding for the night. We stayed at that spot for almost the whole summer. Someone even brought us an old refrigerator that sat in the mud near the tent. We used to joke about it, because it was almost always empty. It also would give you a shock when you grabbed the handle. Paul and I would make a game of it, seeing who could hang on to the handle the longest. Paul would win most of the time. I guess he had something to prove, whereas I didn't feel winning was that important. If there was something in the refrigerator, ma would call Paul to open the door. When it rained, the tent leaked. We would move our blankets to the driest areas possible and make little trenches with sticks to direct the water around us.

The neighbor down the road would let the little kids come over to watch TV. She would sometimes give them something to eat, asking them when was the last time they ate. Her husband hired me to work with him. He was a roofer, and the first thing he did was buy me a pair of sneakers. I didn't even have a decent pair of shoes. He wouldn't let me work without sneakers. I earned about four dollars a day. It was enough to buy a little food. My job was cleaning the roofing from the lawns and eventually carrying roofing to the roof. After a few weeks, the roofer showed me how to lay the roofing.

The four dollars went directly to my father. I never saw the money. I guess he was my agent. Dad made sure I got to sleep at night so I wouldn't be too tired for the next day.

Our meals were spaced out to about one a day. Of course the roofer gave me lunch, which amounted to a sandwich and a glass of water, or a couple times the customer would give me something when we stopped for lunch. I was always hungry. I always had that pain in the pit of my stomach. All our meals at the tent were cooked on an open pit in a pan or kettle. One day we had no food except a bottle of ketchup someone gave us.

When the service was over we stacked the chairs and rolled out our bedding for the night.

Mom heated water on the fire place and poured in the bottle of ketchup. It was late in the day and nearing dusk. She poured a little of the soup into our bowls, and we were enjoying the meal when I noticed around the edge of the bowl little spots scattered like pepper. I thought we had no seasoning, and so I commented on having pepper in the soup. My father stood and came closer to the fire to examine his bowl of soup. Looking at it, he dashed the soup to the ground and turned to us and said, "That's not pepper, it's the gnats from the fire. Quick! Throw it out!" Sure enough, swarming over the fire was about a million gnats. I kept right on eating and told my father if he didn't want to eat that was his business, as for me, I wanted to eat, and I went back for more. Normally I wouldn't eat that way, but when you are hungry you eat things you would not eat.

In that few months I got my share of camping. Some people feel the urge to wrap up their tents, hit the road, and set up a camp somewhere in the wilderness. I did that and don't care to do it again. I did that not because I wanted to get in touch with nature, but nature came up and slapped me in the face.

I really don't mind having hot water from a tap and a toilet I can flush. I thank God every day for the blessings I have. I know what it's like to be hungry and cold and shunned because I was a have-not.

After a while we packed the tent up and started moving again, this time south. I guess my father thought we'd better get into the warm weather before it got really cold. My mother was arguing with my father about us kids getting into a school. It was getting close to September, and we would have to light somewhere soon. We got back into Virginia and the car broke down; it had a busted axle. Dad hitch-hiked to the closest town and was gone for a few hours. He returned with a couple of men who towed the car back with them to town. We stayed in the park there over night; all our things were in the car. The next morning the men returned and informed us the axle was broken. Dad went back with them and returned in the afternoon with the men and an old diamond "T" pick up truck. It was a swap; the hearse for the truck. We went back and got our stuff out of the car and returned to the park that night. Dad got some paint in the deal, and Regina and I painted the truck with brushes. The color was bright royal blue and really looked sharp. We went back to town with the truck and dad got some plywood to enclose the back so we could ride in the back.

West Coast of Florida

We headed south through Georgia to a coastal town in the gulf. The place was Panacea Florida. We stopped in the first church on the main road and found an old man who was a deacon of the church; the church was a Primitive Baptist. The deacon called the pastor, and before long Paul and I were pitching the tent along the main road not far from the church. The people were friendly and helpful. The woman across the street became a Godsend to us. She fed us and helped us all she could, bless her heart. Her name was Dorothy Taylor. There were several young ladies who went to the church and sang in our tent meeting. One of them asked my father if she could marry me. It seemed it was the thing to get married down there at any age over fourteen. I was always hiding out during the day to avoid her. We stayed for about two weeks and our welcome was getting thin. Two days before we left a great storm hit that coast. We scurried into Dorothy's basement, one of only a few in that town, and with us were most of the neighbors. The hurricane was so bad it moved one house across the street. The water in the basement rose to about two feet. Some of the men were crying, and the roar of the wind was deafening. The wind ripped the porch off the house; I can still remember the sound of the nails being pulled out of the house as the porch was torn away. Nobody slept much that night in that basement. There were no lights, and it was cold. I wasn't sure we would survive it. We were four miles from the ocean, and the water had been blown so high it was pouring into the basement. We all did a lot of praying that night.

The next morning we came out of the basement to find the neighborhood completely under water. Two large trees were lying over, the roots protruding from the water.

Everything was flooded. We had to dry out our engine wiring; it took all day to get the old truck running, but when we did we took off, heading north towards Georgia. A second storm was coming right behind the first; into the trip about an hour the storm caught us. We wheeled into Tallassee just after dark. In heavy rain, the town was shaped in a valley, and from one end you could see the other end on the next hill. We stopped for gas and toilet and got right back on the road. I do not believe my father knew where he was going. We were just driving in the night. Early in the morning my father was too tired to go on, and we were forced to stop when he was having trouble keeping the truck on the road. We were in a town called Columbus in the state of Georgia. When we finally woke up and started looking around, our parents decided to try to stay a while. School had already started, and my mother was worried that they would get into some trouble by keeping us out of school.

Columbus, Georgia

Dad made another contact with a church, and we set up the tent in a vacant lot. We had a few meetings and ended up renting a small house in the same neighborhood. The school was about three miles away and there were no school buses. I took my sisters and brothers to the school without our parents. The school officials were confounded at our arrival. The school was a high school, and some of the younger kids had to go to grade school. There was no phone to reach our parents. Finally they took the smaller kids and transported them to the grade school. Regina and I were the only ones that stayed at the high school. The principal escorted us to a room and asked us to sit down for a while and relax. In about an hour he returned to tell us he had received information about our enrollment in Richmond. I asked about Paul, Linda, Maria, and Johnny. He assured me they were in the grade school not far from there. He said we would have to take a test to determine where we should be placed. We were put in separate rooms and given a test of about 500 questions. I thought maybe it was their ninth grade final. They took my test paper when I finished, and in a while the principal appeared and told me Regina did fine and got a 96 on the test. However, my test results were confusing to them. It seemed the test was some sort of an IQ test, and my score was 145, which was too high for my grade level. I thought the test was a little easy, but I didn't say anything to him. Regina was put into class, and I was held for a second test. The second test was a little harder and took a little longer to finish. After they scored it they returned, this time the principal had three people with him. They told me my score was 136.

They wanted to meet my parents right away. I felt the panic of them coming in contact with dad. I asked why but could not get a straight answer. So the principal took me home in his car and came to the front door with me in tow. We stood at the front door, knocking like a couple of Jehovah's witnesses, waiting for my mom to come to the door. To my horror, my father answered the door. He looked at me strangely and then to the principal and asked what was the matter. The principal extended his hand and introduced himself. My father looked at his hand and asked again, "What's this all about? What did he do?"

"It's nothing like that," the man replied, rubbing his unshaken hand with his left hand. "You see, Alfred scored unusually high on our IQ test, and we would like to have him take some other tests."

"So give him another test," my father volunteered. "Well you see, Mister Luckette, that's just it—we would like to send him to Atlanta. His scores are above second year college level, and the university there would like to see him. I called there this morning, after his second test, and they were quite interested in seeing him. We could transport for a few days—"

"Okay, stop right there," my dad interrupted. "I sent my son to school. Just put him in school; he's not going anywhere."

This was the first time I heard about Atlanta and was a little surprised. I could see the anger begin to well up in my father and knew what he would do in a heartbeat. The principal tried to reason for a few minutes but saw the futility in it and resigned his effort, apologized, and backed away from the door.

"As you wish then; I'll enroll him in the tenth grade," he said. When we got back in the car, the principal explained to me about a program offered to some families for a student to get a higher education. He felt that I would fit into the program and could end up starting at Georgia Tech right away. I told him my father would never allow me to go away from the family like that. He said I should try to convince him anyway. The next few weeks the principal would approach me in the school halls and ask if I spoke with my father anymore about Atlanta, and I sheepishly said no luck, but the truth of the matter was I was afraid to even bring it up to him. Dad wouldn't even let me do homework after school in the house. He told one teacher, "You can have him while he's there in school, because it's the law, but when he gets home, he's mine, and I (he would say the I with slow malice, pointing to his chest) will tell him when to stand up and sit down."

One More Trip

Wᴇʟʟ, ᴅᴀᴅ ɢᴏᴛ ɪɴ ᴛʀᴏᴜʙʟᴇ ᴡɪᴛʜ ᴛʜᴇ ʟᴀᴡ ᴛʜᴇʀᴇ ɪɴ Columbus, and Mom found herself alone with eight kids. The county helped us out for a while but told her she should go back to New York. So we made plans to get back. Down the road was a family we came to know. They had two sons who said they would drive us back to New York for gas money and a small fee. One of the boys was recovering from a snake bite in his leg and said he soon would be well enough for the trip.

A couple days before we left, Paul and I stayed out of school to pack for the trip. We had some time and made a huge kite out of newspaper. We painted the kite with some orange paint and took it in the park across the street. The kite was about six feet tall. The wind was perfect; we had the kite up, stretched out over the city. We must have used three or four rolls of twine. The weight of the twine caused the kite to drop to just above the telephone wires. It took all we had to hold the kite. By and by a stranger came up and said, "You boys really have that kite out a long ways."

I turned to the man in the blue suit and said proudly, "We made it ourselves."

"Can I try it?" the man asked. He approached us and took the cord in his hand. We stepped back and watched as the man struggled to hold the kite in check. "It really is a fighter," he said to us as he was being pulled into the wind. "Say boys, where do you go to school?" the man inquired.

"We don't go to school here anymore," Paul piped in then explained that we were leaving tomorrow for New York. The man told us he saw the kite from his office at the school. He was the city truant officer and figured the kite meant kid playing hooky. He pulled the kite in and walked us over to the house where my mother told him it was true about us leaving tomorrow. The officer shook our hands and said good luck to us then said goodbye. He kept the kite.

THE GEORGIA SCHOOL WAS A TRADE SCHOOL. All the classes were designed to train and teach a trade. I had a problem here again because I was a "Yankee." I didn't get into any fights, but I was constantly threatened with bodily harm. The very first day in the auto mechanics class a boy went to the pencil sharpener and began to sharpen his pencil. He made a great deal of sharpening it. Being sure all the class was watching him. Then he turned and blew on the point several times, and approached me. I was sitting in the front row near the teachers desk. He held the pencil close to my face and said, "Hey yank, see this pencil? First chance I get I'm going to stick it in your eye." The teacher just asked him to take his seat, then apologized for his action. That boy never bothered me after that, although, I went out of my way to avoid him. I especially liked the metal class and auto mechanics class. I made a mail box in metal shop, which was a joke because we never got mail. I thought maybe we could hang it on the car somewhere. There were two almost famous teachers there, one was the English teacher named James Cody, a first cousin to William Cody; Wild Bill Cody of the wild west. He really played it up too. He must have been in his seventies and still teaching. The other was the auto mechanics teacher who was Al Capone's chauffer. He told us how he used to drive Capone to Florida from Chicago and around town to the speak-easies. I got a lot of history in his class. He also was an excellent auto mechanic teacher.

You boys really have that kite out a long ways! I turned to the man in the blue suit and said proudly,

Columbus was a hot bed of the civil rights movement at the time. It was right on the Alabama border. The Chattahoochee river separated the cites of Columbus in Georgia and Phoenix City in Alabama. We didn't live too far from the bridge, and Paul and I would walk down and see the shacks along the river where mostly black people lived. They were small huts with boards spaced so you could see right through the huts to the river. We went down there one day because we heard fire engines and police sirens; someone had taken a bus load of blacks on the bridge and shot them. I could not imagine why men hated other men so much. Another time, about two blocks from our house, a seventeen-year-old black boy was chained to a tree near the road and shot to death. The school I attended was a segregated school; the boys there seemed to really hate black people. They would talk of going into the colored neighborhood and shooting them. My mother and I were in the town one day to get some medicine for the baby, Susie, who had a cold. In front of the store was a barrel of axe handles with a sign stating they were to be used to club blacks in language not acceptable in today's world. I was exposed to this hatred and could not understand why men would do this to other people. It was 1960 and the south was deeply divided. Every day we heard about another shooting or killing in the city. I had tasted the hate from both sides of the civil rights issue. The ordeal that I endured in Philadelphia was shocking and terrible. I was beaten almost to death. There were not only the scars on my body, but the mental anguish I endured afterwards. The behavior of those white kids against me was just as bad. I really know what it's like to be hated because of the color of my skin, and where I hail from. God put me there, I believe, to teach me. To love people regardless of what they look like or where they come from. It would be much later when I would read and really understand;

For God so loved the world,
that he gave his only begotten Son,
that whosoever believeth in him
should not perish,
but have everlasting life.
John 3:16 KJB

WE LEFT COLUMBUS WITHOUT DAD. He had to stay. The neighbor boys brought us back to Syracuse. It was a crowded ride of about twenty-three hours. They dropped us off at aunt Millie's in Fairmount. After some hassle and tussle, we ended up in Baldwinsville, New York. We lived between the bridges in a back upstairs apartment. I enrolled in Baker High School and tried to piece my tattered academic studies back together. I had to take biology again because I didn't have the state-required labs, although, I passed the class in Georgia. My other classes had to also be modified to meet the standards of the state. But by the middle of the year I was back in tune with the school requirements. I was back in a friendly environment. No one in the school, not the teachers or students, could understand what I had been through. My sister Regina also recovered academically, but she suffered with other things I could not see nor can I verbalize to this day.

The walk to school was a short walk across the big bridge, up the hill to the high school. I was not in shape for running in the gym, because I never had much of a chance to do the physical stuff, but generally it seemed we were living a somewhat normal life. Up to this point it had seemed as though I was on that rollercoaster for much of my life. All my siblings were riding too. They had their own tales, some of which were horror stories of the worst kind, but we counted ourselves as survivors. We were survivors long before it became a game show.

Minoa

I have not told all the tale; there were things that happened along the way, like I didn't mention all the schools I attended. I dare say I can't remember them and almost none of the names of the people I met. Sometimes things seemed to just fly before me. I can say I lived a life time before I was twelve years old. I went through things that most people will never experience in their whole life. Sometimes when I say I did this or that it seems unbelievable, I sometimes don't want to believe it. But I must, because I was there and did that.

My mother took us kids, when I was sixteen, and moved to Manlius Center, in the same house we lived years before. I entered Minoa High School in the eleventh grade and finished there with a high school diploma. I had gone to Minoa more than any other school I attended. I worked one summer with my uncle Frank, a mechanic, who was an expert on automatic transmissions. He was an articulate mechanic, fussy and sure of his profession. I would disassemble a transmission for him, and he would build it back with needed parts. In his older age he became a Christian and would take me to church with him. The next summer I worked with my uncle Tony DeSantis; he was a home contractor and built many homes in the Fairmount/Solvay areas of Syracuse. He also was a master tradesman, doing most of the construction himself. I remember how we purchased three quarter birch plywood and built kitchen cabinets from scratch. I would level the lawns with a shovel and rake. He treated me like a son.

I met Franny Jo Parker at Minoa; she was a skinny kid. My sister Regina introduced her to me in the auditorium of the school during one of the times the school was called together. They sat up behind me and Regina whispered down that she liked me. I thought it strange; she didn't even know me. I tried to get through school without any involvement with girls but got caught. Maybe not caught, but I needed help in typing a term paper, Franny volunteered to do it. I got to know her. In school we dated a few times then went our separate ways after graduation. One day I was driving along the road and Fran's car was broken down with the hood up on the other side of the street. I turned around, I'm glad I turned around, I pulled up behind her car and got out. "What's the problem?" I asked. She told me it just stopped. I looked it over and offered her a ride home. She accepted and on the way we renewed our acquaintance. I was not dating anyone, and she was only dating occasionally. Later that month I got up the nerve to ask her for a date. She accepted and after that we began a courtship that lead to our marriage.

We had a daughter and were both working. Fran worked in an insurance company in filing, and I was a body repairman, at Centro bus company. We had a babysitter watching Carolyn during the day. The babysitter was having Bible studies in her home on Tuesday nights. The Pastor, Joe Ragonese would conduct the service, and his wife Sue would play the key board. They asked the babysitter to invite Fran and me to the meeting. I refused to go, you see I was racing my car on Sundays. I knew that these Christians met on Sunday. They may meet on Tuesday night, but eventually it boiled down to Sunday, and I was not ready or willing to give up my Sundays. I knew about Jesus, I knew what the Bible taught, but I was too busy to take time out of my schedule. Then the Pastor or his wife started calling our house and tried to invite us to the meeting. I would not respond, I told Fran, tell them I'm not here. Eventually they wore us down to apologetically attend a meeting. I thought to myself *boy is he going to be sorry he invited me*. I came up with about twenty questions, the hardest I could think of about the Word. I put them in my back pocket and went to the meeting.

When we got to the meeting everyone was bubbling over with happiness. They started to sing, and they sang, and sang and sang. I thought they would never get through the singing, and that paper in my pocket was burning. Finally the Pastor opened the Bible and began to read and expound on the word. His words just flowed out, and a strange thing happened. I didn't realize it at first, but he began to hit on some of the questions I was going to ask. As I listened step by step he went over the questions I still had in my back pocket. At the end he asked if I had any questions. He stared straight at me and said, "Al, do you have any questions?" I shook my head, slowly, I was dumbfounded that he answered all twenty questions. "Alright then," he answered, "May I ask you a question? I shrugged and said, "go ahead." "Al, are you ready to accept Christ tonight as you savior?" I looked at Fran, and Pastor Joe said, "uh uh, Al, this is not about Fran, this is something you must do." I looked back at him and shaking my head I said yes. I could not believe I was saying yes but I said it. Then he asked Fran if she wanted to have Jesus as her savior, she also responded in the affirmative.

The Pastor then instructed us to get down on the floor and ask the lord for forgiveness. Fran and I repented of our sins and asked the Lord Jesus to come into our lives and home. We got saved on the kitchen floor in an old farm house. The next week I didn't go to Church. and the week after that I had not planned to go either. I was preparing my car for the race. I came to the car door and placed my hand on the handle. I looked up in the sky and it was a little overcast. Suddenly there was a flash of lightening across the morning sky. I remembered one of the scriptures the pastor spoke on in that meeting.

> *For as the lightning cometh out of the east,*
> *and shineth even unto the west;*
> *so shall also the coming of the Son of man be.*
> Mat 24:27 KJB

I became unnerved, where will I be If he returns? What about my family? I rushed to the house and asked Fran if she wanted to go to Church. She was ready, we took Carolyn and went to church that morning. Everyone was surprised to see us, or at least they acted that way. I haven't missed many services since. The Lord has been Good to me. I traveled around the land, on a long journey with many adventures, but...

If I had to describe who I am, I think I might best say I am the man who was the little boy who lived on Dingle Hole Road.

Conclusion of the Matter

As I REFLECT BACK INTO MY EARLY CHILDHOOD, I NOW SEE how the Lord helped me survive. At least twice, death was at my door, once with disease at age twelve and another time in a physical attack on me in the city of Philadelphia when I was fifteen. I learned about discipline and patience and dealing with rejection. I saw how men dealt with each other and treated one another. It was as if the Lord took this small boy from the rural suburbs of upstate New York and allowed him to experience the feelings of others.

The civil rights movement in America would mean nothing to me if I had remained on the farm. My father was neutral, or oblivious, to the raging war of equality. He always told me to not get involved in other people's affairs. I could have grown to look the other way or even become someone who hated men because of the color of their skin. I saw what happened when there were no moral values applied or given to men. I also saw misappropriated moral values, and how men used God to direct their hate towards other men. I was tempered by both arguments of that fight. I hear some men today use their past as a reason for their hatred or poverty or even their lack of morality, but it won't work with me. God helped me to overcome all the obstacles of my past and showed me what I would be without Him. It is because God loved us that we are saved, and this love is extended through us to all men. As the scripture says, "Beloved, let us love one another."

Some, indeed most of the things I have written about here concerning my experiences, are lessons in humility, temperance, meekness, and faith. A few of the experiences show my lack of humility when faced with bigotry. When the coach refused to let Paul and me join the scouts, we answered with war and hatred. God showed me later how people would treat me because I was white, just as we treated those boys who wore scout uniforms and were not necessarily of the same mind as that coach. When I was faced with the almost impossible task of sorting piles of shoes, I see God sorting men on the Day of Judgment. When our car burned to the ground on Christmas day, I saw the people rally to help us, take us in, and feed us, just as God takes in those who are wrecked and ruined on the highway of life. My life on the road was like that of a pilgrim, one traveling from place to place with no permanent home, but in the end I got a home and a family, just as God will give all pilgrims of this life a home and Family.

Some of the things that happened to me were tragic and fearful. I thought I would never overcome the thought of them. But now I can laugh at the experience, sometimes uncontrollably. You may have had some things that happened in your past, some things even worse than what I experienced. I often quote this passage from the Apostle Paul who said,

"There hath no temptation taken you
but such as is common to man:
but God *is* faithful,
who will not suffer you to be tempted
above that ye are able;
but will with the temptation
also make a way to escape,
that ye may be able to bear *it*." (KJB)

Isn't that great?

The Lord gave me a ministry in song and preaching. My past serves as a reminder of his love for me. The following are some of the poems I wrote. I hope they bless you as they bless me. Many of them have had a melody added, and we sing them from time to time in our church. Now may the Lord Jesus richly bless you, your home, your family, and all your endeavors, may He enrich your understanding of Him. May the Lord empower you to live a life pleasing to Him, that you may become an overcomer and blessing to all. In Jesus precious Name.

I am One of Those

We're often called peculiar and different in this day.
The things we did before are vanishing away;
Jesus changed my being, from my
head down to my toes.
I used to be a sinner, but now I'm one of those.

Spoke to a man last week; he told me to slow down.
You ought to keep your religion
and not spread it around;
And all the things you say, well Heaven only knows,
But I have to shout it out, because
I am one of those.

You get a funny look, and then
they shake their head.
You realize that it must be something that you said;
Then they stumble for a word,
knowing they're your foes.
And with their nose held high, they
say, "Oh, you're one of those."

Yes, I'm a chosen person,
Hand picked by God's own Son.
And since He came unto me,

The Devil's on the run.
My Savior's living with me

and scatters all my woes.
And I can tell you gladly,
Yes, I am one of those.

8-7-91

Know ye not that the unrighteous shall not inherit the kingdom of God? Be not deceived: neither fornicators, nor idolaters, nor adulterers, nor effeminate, nor abusers of themselves with mankind, Nor thieves, nor covetous, nor drunkards, nor revilers, nor extortioners, shall inherit the kingdom of God. And such were some of you: but ye are washed, but ye are sanctified, but ye are justified in the name of the Lord Jesus, and by the Spirit of our God. 1 Cor. 6:9–11(KJB)

My song is Jesus

I won't be moved by earthly charm.
My song is Jesus.
When trials press, there's no alarm.
My song is Jesus.

My melody will always sing his praise.
Complete in him I'll gladly run this race.
Someday at Heaven's gate, I'll see his face.
My song is Jesus, My song is Jesus.

I will not change this blessed refrain.
My song is Jesus.
There's nothing else that I can gain;
My song is Jesus.

The world sings another tune.
My song is Jesus.
Their song will only bring them ruin;
My song is Jesus.

Together all our voices ring,
My song is Jesus.
The church redeemed this chorus sing;
My song is Jesus.

3-14-88

Saying, I will declare thy name unto my brethren, in the midst of the church will I sing praise unto thee. Heb 2:12 (KJB)

Sunday morning

Sunday is the best day
For me since I got saved.
That's when Saints do gather
and worship in a rave.
On Sunday you can find me
standing joyfully at my pew,
singing praise to Heaven
for making me brand new!

Wednesday we do gather
and study God's good word,
praying for the wisdom
to do what we have heard.
But then there comes a Sunday,
when the Saints do sing aloud,
reminds me of the rapture
and the meeting in the clouds.

9-6-88

Not forsaking the assembling of ourselves together,
as the manner of some *is;* but exhorting *one another:* and
so much the more, as ye see the day approaching. Heb.
10:25(KJB)

The preaching of the word

I love to hear a man of God
Expound in spiritual phrase.
To call us out from bondage tight,
And fear in these last days.

Our faith can grow by listening
As God pricks our hearts within
And admonishes us to turn about,
Repenting of all our sin.

Our faith in Christ is not increased
By seeing sick folk cured
But lending ears and hearts alike,
To the preaching of the Word!

9-7-88

How then shall they call on him in whom they have
not believed? and how shall they believe in him of whom
they have not heard? and how shall they hear without a
preacher? Rom. 10:14(KGB)

Jesus Will See You Through

Four anchors of hope will hold you, my friend,
As you travel this life's stormy sea.
They'll help you, support you;
I know that they will
Because I know what they've done for me.

Take *courage,* my friend,
And *trust* in the Lord.
Have *hope* in his promises too,
And *patiently stand* as a child of the King,
And Jesus will see you through.

Step out in faith and fear not the blast
That the enemy may bring your way.
Have courage in Christ
And watch day and night,
And don't forget to pray.

6-11-84

Then fearing lest we should have fallen upon rocks, they cast four anchors out of the stern, and wished for the day. Acts 27:29(KJB)

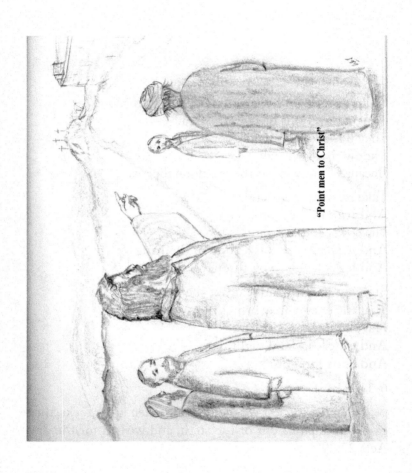

"Point men to Christ"

Prepare Yourself

When we read our paper, there's trouble all around.
War and famine plague us and earthquakes shake the ground.
They kill their little babies before they leave the womb;
Prepare yourself, prepare yourself,
He's coming very soon.

The Master prophesied about these days so dark.
He said remember Noah and why he built the Ark.
The evil that you're seeing is only one more sign;
Prepare yourself, prepare yourself,
Your soul is on the line.

Prepare yourself, my friend, don't think that your so bold.
You may live to ninety-nine and have this world's gold;
But then what does it profit to leave it all behind;
Prepare yourself prepare yourself,
Your soul is on the line.

Prepare yourself; it's later than you think.
Prepare yourself; your on the very brink.
The time goes by as quickly as a wink.
Prepare yourself, prepare yourself,
It's later than you think.

And this know, that if the goodman of the house had known what hour the thief would come, he would have watched, and not have suffered his house to be broken through. Be ye therefore ready also: for the Son of man cometh at an hour when ye think not. Luke 12:39,40(KJB)

Jesus is the Only Way

Jesus is the only way.
He's the only name you'll
Hear on that day.
What price will you bring
When you stand before
The King?
Jesus is the only way.

Jesus is the only way,
And he walked upon the
The water one sweet day.
He healed the blind and lame;
All glory to his name.
Jesus is the only way.

Jesus is the only way.
He's the truth and the life;
I'm here to say.
He gave his life for me
On the cross of Calvary.
Jesus is the only way.

Jesus saith unto him, *I am the way, the truth, and the life:
no man cometh unto the Father, but by me.* John 14:6(KJB)

What Does it Profit

What does it profit, I must ask,
To gain the world; a mighty task.
Then after all is on your side,
Go to Hell and there abide.
If you should live past ninety and nine
With worldly riches and think it fine,
And if you tasted this world's fame,
What does it profit, where is your gain?
Can you exchange all these worldly pleasures
For even one of Heaven's treasures?
Chose you this day, Christ Jesus King,
Or keep to you what this life will bring.
He offers life eternal. Free;
He paid it all at Calvary.
There is no way you can compare
What we have here with what we have there!

7-6-87

Lord, Carry Me

I know the promises of God are really true,
And I'm going to a city that's brand new;
You won't find any trouble in that land,
But for this next mile, I'll need a helping hand.

Trials are something we all go through,
And the best of us will have to face a few.
When they get me down and no on seems to care,
And the weight of it is more than I can bear,

I call on Jesus. Come and set me free,
Jesus, carry me this time, I plea.
I don't think I can make it without you.
Lord, carry me for just a mile or two.

10-10-93

Where Your Treasure is, Your Heart Will Be

In the Bible we read of a rich man
Who tore all his barns to the ground.
I'll build me some that are bigger;
I'll have the best all around.

But an angel came to collect him.
God required his soul that night;
Those barns will belong to another,
No Heavenly treasure in sight.

Where your treasure is, your heart will be.
Where your treasure is, your heart will be.
Are you storing a treasure in Heaven above?
Have you made a deposit at the bank of love?

In the bible we read of a poor man
Who had no barns to tear down.
He didn't eat at the rich man's table,
And the dogs licked his sores all around.
And an Angel came to collect him
And carried him off that night.
To a treasure he'd stored up in Heaven,
Now we know that the poor mans all right.

8-26-95

182

The Rich man and the begger, Lazarus

Luke 16:20

Luk 16:24
And he cried and said,
Father Abraham, have
mercy on me, and send
Lazarus, that he may dip
the tip of his finger in water,
and cool my tongue; for I am
tormented in this flame.

A Million Years From Now

I'm happy, can't you see. My savior's pardoned me.
He's taken all my sins away; I've life eternally.
He's washed me in His blood. He's washed me in
His blood.
He changed my heart, renewed my mind;
Oh what a cleansing flood.

In the twinkling of an eye I'll meet him in the sky;
I'll ride the clouds with the Angels there,
In the twinkling of an eye.
A million years from now, a million years from now;
I'll still have Jesus for my friend, a million years from now.

10-4-95

Forgive

When you come to Jesus and ask him to forgive you,
Did you know there are conditions you must meet?
Did you know that in order to be forgiven,
You must forgive, and lay it at His feet?

Do you find it hard to say 'I'm sorry'
When others you defame along this way?
Don't you know that Jesus won't forgive you;
Your sin remains, and for those sins you'll pay.

Forgive, so you can be forgiven
Forgive; just let it drop away.
Forgive, and you will be forgiven.
These words of life I give to you this day.

Do you find it hard to say 'I'm sorry'
When others you defame along this way?;
Don't you know that Jesus won't forgive you?
Forgive and let the savior in today.

10-11-95

And when ye stand praying, forgive, if ye have ought against any: that your Father also which is in heaven may forgive you your trespasses. But if ye do not forgive, neither will your Father which is in heaven forgive your trespasses.

Mark 11:25,26(KJB)

Voice in the Wilderness

In those days came John the Baptist,
Preaching in that wilderness land,
And he said, "Repent all you people,
For the kingdom of heaven is at hand."

The voice of one crying in the wilderness;
Prepare the way, prepare ye the way.
Make straight His paths, repent or perish
This was John's message for the people of that day.

He wore a coat of camel hair;
A leather girdle around his waist,
And his meat was locusts and wild honey.
The greatest prophet that that nation ever faced.

In these last days we hear the message.
We're preaching in this wilderness land;
It's still repent, all you people,
For the kingdom of Heaven is at hand.

3-1-94

Mat 3:1 In those days came John the Baptist, preaching in the wilderness of Judaea,

My Storm

Tempest strong against my face
as I press on towards Heaven's place,
clouds so dark they hide the sun.
Can't see ahead, but I must run.
What is this weight that clings to me?
Pulling me down; I must get free.
I feel the rain, it stings my brow.
I must press on, Heaven's gate somehow,
But there beside me, someone I'm free.
The burden I'm hauling, lightened from me;
Now spring forward, my helper near,
I'll make it in spite of all my fear.
There, just ahead, I hear bells ringing,
Come with me, through this storm singing.

6-29-87

Are we growing?

For when for the time ye ought to be teachers, ye have need that one
teach you again which be the first principles of the oracles of God;
and are become such as have need of milk, and not of strong meat.

Hebrews 5: 12 KJB

Little baby wipe his nose, will he ever learn, do you suppose?
Stumbles along carnal in mind, look back and see... two steps behind.
Are we growing?

Ask all the people, read your bible, God will call, and make you liable;
One verse here, another tomorrow, trouble comes, and here comes sorrow.
Are we growing?

But they enjoy the world's pleasure, spend all their time. That's their treasure,
What, do you want me to have no fun? I'm only human, so let me run.
Are we growing?

They've been in Christ for thirty years, no growing pains, they've shed no tears,

Gave no place for spiritual things, the world's bell is all that rings.
Are we growing?

These little babies want to teach, you can have it all, it's in your reach,
That's what they tell you one and all, but in their trial they slip and fall.
Are we growing?

AEL 05/88

Back home

*And not many days after
the younger son gathered all together,
and took his journey into a far country,
and there wasted his substance with riotous living.*

Luke 15:13 KJB

There is a story in my bible book,
Of a son who one day a Journey took;
A loving father he left behind,
He told his dad, I want what's mine.

And so he journeyed to a country far,
And spent his worth across the bar;
he fed the pigs on husks of corn,
himself he thought why was I born.

Starving at a farm he pondered,
why from my father have I wandered;
there's food a plenty at that home,
why did I ever want to roam.

I'll return and earn my pay,
I'll go back I know the way;
I'll tell my dad I'm sorry too,
Please let me come and live with you.

The story book gives record true,
That young man started out anew;

As he approached the home he missed,
His father met him with a kiss.

God the father is like this dad,
He knows your past is filled with bad;
He waits for you at your hearts door,
With shoes and rings and so much more.

Can we meet at heaven's gate?
Come along don't hesitate;
A little prayer, is all we need,
And Jesus blood is all we plead.

Like the son that left his home,
You and I did also roam;
We were afar because of sin,
But now by grace we've entered in.

AEL07/01/13

Baptize me

And Philip said, If thou believest with all thine heart, thou mayest. And he answered and said, I believe that Jesus Christ is the Son of God. Acts 8:37 KJB

Phillip on the Gaza road, met a eunuch in despair;
Reading Holy Scriptures not knowing how he'd fare;
Philip asked him truly, "Do you understand"
The man replied, "No sir, I need a helping hand."

Chorus: I'm going down to the water,
            With Jesus on my mind;
               I'm calling, please Holy Spirit
            fill this heart of mine,
               I'm going down to the water,
            with Jesus on my mind;
               I've got Jesus, Jesus on my mind.

Philip gave the gospel message on that old and dusty road,
To a man who went to worship, he freed his heavy load;
If you believe, with all your heart, Philip told him true;
We'll get off this chariot, go down and baptize you.

Now if you're on a dusty road, and your heart is parched with sin;
come down to the water, you can jump right in;
Open up your stony heart, the Savior beckons you,

you'll be born again,
and start a life brand new!

AEL 04/03/90

Phillip meet the unuech on the Gaza road
ACTS Chap. 8 26-38

Busy

Redeeming the time, because the days are evil.

Ephesians 5:16

No one likes a lazy man,
Who never sets a goal;
No one likes a wealthy man,
Who puts his money in a hole.

But what about a busy man,
Who always has no time;
A busy man you can not reach,
Oh what an awful crime.

Ask him if he has the time,
To help you cut the grass;
Oh not today, I'm busy now,
Fraid I'll have to pass,

Ask him if he has the time,
To go to church today;
Sorry I'm to busy now,
the Yankees are to play.

you ask him if he has some time,
you'd like to share the word;
come back tomorrow after noon,
how often have you heard.

If only you could slow him down,
And hold him by the sleeve;
And tell him Jesus loves him,
Before he has to leave.

The lazy man is hard to reach,
At least that's what I'm told;
The wealthy man has locked the door,
His heart is something cold.

But I think the rich and lazy,
Are easier to reach;
than one too busy here on earth,
to listen to you preach.

If you have a busy life,
And you're trying to win a race;
Stop! Repent! Call on God,
And try to slow your pace.

We're only given so much time,
to pilgrim in this life;
to have a job, and build a house,
and argue with a wife.

When all is said my busy friend,
While it is called today;
Ask Jesus in to you heart,
That's all I have to say.

AEL07\05\13

Called out

But the God of all grace, who hath called us unto his eternal glory by Christ Jesus, after that ye have suffered a while, make you perfect, stablish, strengthen, settle you.

1Peter 5:10 KJB

I walked alone, no friend was near,
A lonely road of pain and fear; .
Then a voice called out, "come unto me,"
I rushed to Him, and now I'm free.

Called out, I've heard my name,
Called out, from sin and shame;
All my past life is left behind,
He called me out and renewed my mind.

A voice is calling, for you today,
His beckon cry says don't delay;
Why should you share in the sins of men?
Come out from bondage, be born again.

06/07/90 AEL

Church people

*Behold, how good and how pleasant it is
for brethren to dwell together in unity!*

Psalms 133:1 KJB

What loving people in this church,
We sing and pray and on chairs we perch;
We meet most Wednesdays just after seven,
And talk about the Lord and Heaven.

When pastor Din says, your song now,
Brother Ken gets up, I don't know how;
And leads us in thou art worthy,
Then back to his seat we see him scurry.

One will pick their favorite song
And all of us will sing along
All the songs are in our book,
We know them all without a look.

Now there's the song that Roger chooses,
We're all awake and no one snoozes;
But he finds a song we haven't heard,
We scratch our heads at every word.

such a pretty song with words of power,
we learned the tune within the hour;
now when Pastor calls out "Rogers song,"
the congregation chimes along.

Back in the corner a willing hand,
Is David sitting with his fan;
For God's word his heart does burn,
As he is looking for the Lord's return.

Our piano player knows the keys,
she really makes the ivories tease;
she must have studied late and long,
to help us praise the Lord in song.

Andy Bunton takes the lead,
And brings a study yes indeed;
We dig into the word and pray,
That we will see the Lord one Day.

AEL. 07/01/13

Do you believe Jesus

That if thou shalt confess with thy mouth
the Lord Jesus, and shalt believe in thine heart that
God hath raised him from the dead, thou shalt be saved.
                                                            Romans 10:9 KJB

He calmed the sea; He walked on the water;
He healed the sick, raised Jairus' daughter;
> The words He spoke,
> Brought life to the dead;
> And he's coming back,
> In the bible it's said.

Do you believe Jesus?
A friend that is true,
Do you believe Jesus?
He'll see you through;
He breaks the chains of, fear and doubt,
Do you believe Jesus? He's calling you out.

My loving Savior has a loving name,
He cast out demons, He healed the lame;
> He pulled my soul
> From the threat of Hell;
> He healed my being,
> And made me well.
>   08/20/88 AEL

Double mindedness

*Draw nigh to God, and he
will draw nigh to you. Cleanse your
hands, ye sinners; and purify your
hearts, ye double minded.*

James 4:8 KJB

A man once said he'd make it up to Heaven,
Said he always had a (very) lucky streak;
He said, "I never worry or get bothered,
'cause I'm a lucky guy when things get bleak.

But......
A double minded man can't win this battle;
It takes more than luck to come out on the top;
The devil wants to take you down to Hell,
And you'll need more than luck to make him stop.

A girl back home once told me, friend, I hear ya,
But your preaching here won't help me out at all;
"cause I'm going up to Heaven 'cause I'm lucky,
And lucky people slip, but they don't fall.

But......
A double minded man can't win this battle;
It takes more than luck to come out on the top;
The devil wants to take you down to Hell,
And you'll need more than luck to make him stop.

Now Jesus said, "come and bring your burdens,"
This life you find is often filled with strife;
Don't hide yourself in thinking luck can help you,
Only Jesus can supply eternal life.

10/10/91 AEL ©

Foolish little thoughts

The thought of foolishness is sin:
and the scorner is an abomination to men.

Proverbs 24:9

A foolish thought is like the planting of a weed,
as it grows it overcomes the other garden seed;
Trouble comes from every corner by that foolish little thought,
and all is lost of all the wisdom we had ever sought.

Entangled in our faith that foolish thought will grow,
and reaching its maturity chokes out what we should know;
If only we could learn to pluck that foolish little seed,
we'd live and grow so happily and on God's word we'd feed.

Rebuke that foolish thought, the seed of Satan's crop;
It has no place for people who place God at the top;
We're growing in the Savior, our wisdom's from above,
we're living in his Spirit, while walking in His love.

So when you get a foolish thought, rebuke it in His Name,
cast it out from you, don't play the Devil's game;
Your faith in God is increased by the reading of His word;
And there you'll find the greatest wisdom that you have ever heard.!

06/05/88 AEL ©

Gossip

If you spread a story
you have heard,
Which does not have a lifting word;

It will haunt you, yes it can,
Gossip can land you in the frying pan.

Al Luckette 08/28/2004

He rescued me

And I know the Lord is good,
He always told me that He would,
Take care of all my needs and strengthen me;
So I trust Him yes I do,
In this Pilgrim land He's true,
Jesus yes Jesus rescued me.

He rescued me
From troubled water,
He rescued me
And now I'm free;
He rescued me
And I do love Him;
Jesus yes Jesus rescued me.

Now when trouble comes my way,
I call on Jesus and I say,
Oh! Jesus fill my heart and set me free;
With that Holy Spirit blast,
From my being fear is cast;
Jesus yes Jesus rescued me.

When you stumble in this land,
And can't find a helping hand;
Call on Jesus he can catch you when you fall;
Never fear the storm or dark,
'cause you're riding in God's ark,
Jesus yes Jesus rescues all.

Then said Daniel unto the king, O king, live for ever. My God hath sent his angel, and hath shut the lions' mouths, that they have not hurt me: forasmuch as before him innocency was found in me; and also before thee, O king, have I done no hurt.   Daniel 6:21,22

He wrote my name in the sand

This they said, tempting him, that they might have to accuse him. But Jesus stooped down, and with his finger wrote on the ground, as though he heard them not.

John 8:6 KJB

I was a pretty good Joe, I never hurt anyone,
I liked to go to town, and I liked to have some fun;
But like the woman in the bible that was caught in her sin,
I came to realize you have to pay for what you've been.

So I looked down in the dirt, where the master knelt,
He was tugging at my heart; I didn't know what I felt;
The crowd was screaming, but I just watched his hand,
there before my eyes, he wrote my name in the sand.

He wrote my name in the sand,
He wrote my name in the sand;
I thought I was a pretty good man,
But it was my name He wrote in the sand.

I got down on my knees and I asked Him in,
I knew from that moment he'd forgiven my sin;
My life's been changed, I haven't any strife,
now my name is written in the Lamb's book of life.

When you point your finger at another man,
you can't see the sin that's in your hand;

Jesus stooped down and he wrote your name;
He wrote your name in the sand.

03/03/89 AEL

Heavenly trip.

*For the Lord himself shall descend
from heaven with a shout, with the voice of
the archangel, and with the trump of God:
and the dead in Christ shall rise first:*

1 Thessalonians 4:16

Thinking about my transportation,
Will it be a teleportation?
The bridegroom comes by obligation,
the whole world will be in exasperation

One day we'll hear the trumpet sound,
When Jesus comes with clouds around;
And gathers men like wheat and hay,
While angels watch that blessed day.

The bride groom comes at early dawn,
And This mortal flesh will all be gone;
No sores or pain can enter in
Neither can a trace of sin.

The graves will open of the Saints.
But all is quiet among the ain'ts;
White robes will be worn on that day,
Shouts and praise along the way.

Al Luckette 07/01/13

We will meet with tears of Joy

I've got Resurrection living in my soul

Know ye not that ye are the temple of God, and that the Spirit of God dwelleth in you?

1 Corinthians 3:16 KJB

He came into my heart and made me whole,
Eternal life and Jesus is my goal;
Now my name is written on that roll,
'cause I've got Resurrection living in my soul.

He's the one who took my sin away,
When he suffered on the cross that day;
Now my name is written on that roll,
'cause I've got Resurrection living in my soul.

I've got Resurrection living in my soul.
I've got Resurrection living in my soul.
Now my name is written on that roll,
'cause I've got Resurrection living in my soul.

Now I've been chosen to be a son,
Since I got saved the Devil's on the run;
Now my name is written on that roll,
'cause I've got Resurrection living in my soul.

The things I did before I've laid aside,
And on the word of God I will abide;
Now my name is written on that roll,
'cause I've got Resurrection living in my soul.

AEL. 11/01/1995

I must be somebody special

*But ye are a chosen generation, a royal priesthood,
an holy nation, a peculiar people; that ye should
shew forth the praises of him who hath called you
out of darkness into his marvelous light;*

1 Peter 2:9 KJB

I've got no riches to offer,
no talent I'd call my own;
Yet Jesus suffered on Calvary,
for my sins He died to atone.

I must be somebody special,
To the Master who reigneth above;
I must be someone important,
'else why would He show me this love?

My life was filled with disorder,
I never'd do anything right,
Then Jesus came knocking on my door,
Now all of my burdens are light.

Not bought with silver or gold,
or fineries found in this land;
But by the Blood of His Son,
For He has made me a new Man.

04/07/89 AEL

I will never leave Thee.

Let your conversation be without covetousness;
and be content with such things as ye have: for
he hath said, I will never leave thee, nor forsake thee.
Hebrews 13:5 KJB

I will never leave you, nor will I forsake thee,
seek me and I'll be found among my friends;
Ask now and I will answer when you call.

> For I will never leave thee,
> No I will never leave thee.

And in my strength and power you won't fall
> For I will never leave thee,
> I will never leave thee,
> I will never leave thee.
> 05/10/92 AEL ©

Is your heart set on things Heavenly?

*Set your affection on things above,
not on things on the earth. Col 3:2*

Is your heart set on things Heavenly?
Are you sold out to Jesus thoroughly?
When you speak to friends each day,
Do you tell them he's the way?
Is your heart set on things Heavenly?

As you pilgrim through this land of many trials,
Often you may stumble on the way;
So at sunset, when you lay your head down,
Ask Jesus to forgive your sins this day.

Is your heart set on things Heavenly?
Are you sold out to Jesus thoroughly?
When you go to bed at night,
Do you say more than good night?
Is your heart set on things Heavenly?

01/05/96 AEL

Jack

As the young man strolled on the sidewalk along,
He counted the cracks and whistled a song;
Up ahead an old friend coming his way,
It's Jack who always has something to say.

Now Jack is a poor man not much to his name,
He hasn't much money, and walks with a cane;
He's lived in the hood, for most of his life,
Down near the bridge with three kids and a wife;
He worked in the factory, till it had shut down,
Now he hobbles along, all over the town.

The young man who's name is Al Luckette,
Is wiping his brow because of his sweat;
Quite a hot day, Al says to old Jack,
As he touches the man with a pat on his back.

Jack looks around, ah what a beautiful day,
Your just in time to hear what I'll say;
before Al could speak Jack lifted his cane,
and waved to the people walking the lane.

When ever Jack spoke his cane he would wave,
Jack always spoke of the Lord with a rave;
The crowds gathered round, to hear poor Jack,
Call on his God and in spite of his lack.

The Lord called on Noah, Jack lifted his voice,
God calls on men, and gives them a choice;
Get into the ark, Jack waved his old cane,
I'm shutting the door, and sending the rain.

The wickedness then had filled the whole earth,
And suddenly Jack turned, and spoke of new birth;
You can't go to heaven, he said to the crowd,
Without the new birth, he shouted aloud.

The riches you have, won't do you no good,
Jack limped a little forward from the place where he stood;
Pointing his cane at the Heaven above,
He told them they needed the gift of God's Love.

As the time passed along, Jack spoke of God's grace
And how men like him would finish the race;
Some in the crowd ask the Lord to come in,
As they went to their knees, in forgiveness of sin.

Now Jack turned around with a grin and a prayer,
Cause he knew that God's Spirit was with him out there;
I've only one life and soon I'll be gone,
But I'll be with Jesus, just before dawn.

That night as the owl hooted up in a tree,
the Angels of God let Jack's spirit free;
his wife and his kids will miss ol' Jack,
but they know some day he will be back.

AEL 07\04\13

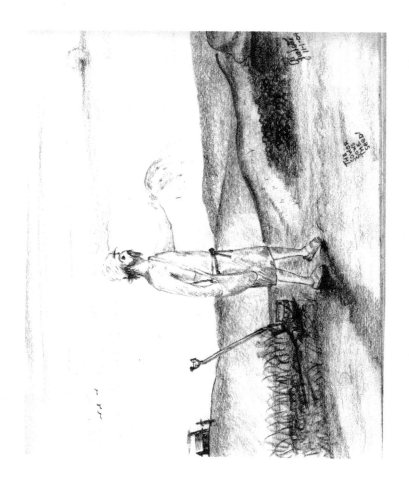

JUST ANOTHER DAY

Behold, I shew you a mystery; We shall not all sleep, but we shall all be changed,
In a moment, in the twinkling of an eye, at the last trump: for the trumpet shall sound,
and the dead shall be raised incorruptible, and we shall be changed.
For this corruptible must put on incorruption, and this mortal must put on immortality.

1 Cor. 15: 51–53

Therefore be ye also ready: for in such an hour as ye think not the Son of man cometh.

Matt 24:44

Today is just another day, the market's in a bustle,
People rushing here and there, my there's quite a hustle;
Some are going to the church today, a marriage there I think,
All the pomp and famous ones are gathered for a drink;
The sun is shining, not a cloud, a pleasant day I'd say,
Time to walk the dog around, or take nine holes today.

I heard that some are planning, a weekend at the lake,
And the church on Genesee, is planning for a bake;
Oh just around the corner, Christmas on the way,
More shopping, singing, having fun, It's just another day.

But there's something different in the air, a quiet sort
of breeze,
It says to watch and pray, be ready if you please;
Then there that strange small cloud, rising from the east,
Closer, closer comes the cloud, upon these men who feast;
And there, it looks like, oh no I'm sure it can not be
A man standing in the cloud, what is this my eyes do see.

Now I hear a blast so loud, I cover up my ears,
That trumpet sound has touched my soul, and brought my
eyes to tears;
A million Angels suddenly appear, and fill the morning sky,
I beat my breast and cry aloud, and in my heart a heavy sigh;
I see the graves are broken up, and bodies coming out,
They are going up and singing too, what is this all about?

Some I know in less a time, before my eye could twinkle,
Are dressed in white and taken up, they have no spot
or wrinkle;
The sadness of the moment, I'm overcome with fear,
The Lamb has come and taken home the church He
loves so dear;

They told me to be ready; I thought I had some time,
To live my life, and take a wife, and even spend my dime;
How foolish now it seems to me, to miss this faithful call,
For just a passing fancy, I'm sure I missed it all;

Oh how often did they beg me, to ask the savior in?
But I would tell them later on, I'll repent of all my sin;
And they would tell the story, He's coming back, they'd say,
But I didn't think that He would come, on just another day!

AEL 12/11/90

Life

The one who's true
Repentance, blue,
Strong mighty wind,
Mourn for sin,
Living in din,
Where've I been,
High places ride,
Taken aside,
road narrow, flight,
no left no right,
cleaned up, inside,
in him abide,
living in might,
given small light,
rock of all ages,
lost all my rages,
what have I heard,
attend to the word,
sweep out the dust,
goodbye old lust;
ashes away,
new life every day,
take up thy cross
gather no moss,
cheer to each friend,

good words must lend,
that day shall appear,
wiped from all fear,
live now below,
but life's all aglow,
someday tho.. I'll see,
Heaven's gate there I'll be.

AEL.

No one can pluck me out of his hand

My sheep hear my voice, and I know them, and they follow me: And I give unto them eternal life; and they shall never perish, neither shall any man pluck them out of my hand.

John 10: 27–28

I heard a knock at my hearts door,
Jesus said I'll give you life forever more;
My heart was flooded with his love and grace;
When Jesus came, my sins he did erase.

The world wars against me every day,
And often, my flesh gets in the way;
Sometimes I seem to waver in this fight;
Then Jesus comes and makes my burdens light.

The journey through this life is often hard,
But the spirit in my heart is keeping guard
The devil wants to drag me down to Hell;
But Jesus touched my life and made me well

No one can pluck me out of his hand,
No one can pluck me out of his hand;
I hear his voice and follow his commands;
And no one can pluck me out of his hand.

No one can pluck you out of his hand,
No one can pluck you out of his hand;
If you hear his voice, and follow his command,
Then no one can pluck you out of his hand.

AEL.01-10-2016

Noah and the Ark

But of that day and hour knoweth no man,
no, not the angels of heaven, but my Father only.
But as the days of Noe were, so shall also the
coming of the Son of man be.

Mat 24:36,37 KJB

There was an ark so long ago,
And men were running to and fro;
They wouldn't enter to be saved,
Instead they mocked, in riotous rave;
So Noah took his family few,
His three sons became the crew;
And two by two the critters came,
And got in out of God's heavy rain.

The waters rose above the earth,
While back in town there was no mirth;
Man and child died that day,
The wrath of God on earth did prey;
Only eight survived the flood,
The rest were left in earthly mud;
This reminder to young and old,
Don't covet silver and precious gold.

Two sides of God that we can see,
One of love for you and me;
But the other side contains His wrath,
So find the straight and narrow path;
Accept His helping hand today,
Come to His side while you may;
Judgment day is not far off,
And God will punish all who scoff.

Jesus is coming to visit this earth
For those who have the second birth;
Weeping and wailing, for those in the dark,
Quick, the door is closing, get into the ark.

AEL

Noah

By faith Noah, being warned of God of things not seen as yet, moved with fear, prepared an ark to the saving of his house; by the which he condemned the world, and became heir of the righteousness which is by faith.

Hebrews 11:7 KJB

The Ark was built by Noah, an amateur indeed,
Titanic by the pros, it sunk and so we read;
They built their fated vessel at dock close to the sea,
And slipped it into the water, for everyone to see.

But Noah built his Ark, way up on a mountain top,
And crowds would come to visit to laugh and even mock;
Noah had the faith, in God's salvation plan;
The water rose and lifted him, off from the grassy land.

He preached and preached, to all the wicked men;
He told them to get ready, but they laughed at him instead;
One lesson we must not forget, Noah's ark did easily float;
And if you want to save your life, don't ever miss the boat.
AEL. 05/05/2017

PETER AND THE MASTER

Now as he walked by the sea of Galilee,
he saw Simon and Andrew his brother
casting a net into the sea: for they were fishers.

Mark 1:16 KJB

Another day out to sea, we never get enough,
Didn't catch too much last night, the sea was kind of rough;
Ah, I love the sea, and love to fish, the sea is good to me,
My dad, and friends were fishermen, it's what I always
knew I'd be:
There's quite a stir at Jordan's banks, the Baptist is in town,
We all went down to hear him preach, and many
came around:
He said there was one coming, mightier than he,
Could this be the holy one? We'll have to wait and see.

Andrew says we should return, and hear this Baptist talk
And more about this holy one, It's just a little walk.
We ought to fish, I said it's where we need to go
But there we were, down at the river, brother Andrew had
me in tow:
The Baptist just began to preach, he really moved the crowd
When suddenly, he pointed to a man, as he did cry aloud;
Behold the LAMB of God that takes our sin away,
I'm glad I listened to my brother, on that special day,

AEL. 07/05/2014

Sleepy world

I beseech you therefore, brethren, by the mercies of God,
that ye present your bodies a living sacrifice, holy,
acceptable unto God, which is your reasonable service.
And be not conformed to this world: but be ye transformed
by the renewing of your mind, that ye may prove what is
that good, and acceptable, and perfect, will of God.

Romans 12: 1,2 KJB

Sleepy world, closed up eyes,
Turns it's face, won't arise;
See their sins, and filthy style,
They look away, at their dung pile;
Can't let go, it's all they got,
Worked so hard for that dung plot;
Bondage hard, by Satan's hand,
Sin looks good, in this poor land.
Worldly cares, and costly riches,
Is what they seek, to ease their itches;
The chain of custom, holds them down;
Makes them look like Satan's clown.
But freedom's come for all today,
Christ's shed blood for sin to pay,
Let go of the Devil, to live his Hell,
Ask Jesus in, He'll make you well;
Remove desires to follow the old,

Makes you new, makes you bold;
Temptations rush in a mighty flood,
But no sweat, your covered by Jesus precious blood.
Choose you this day, Satan's strife,
Or trust in Christ, and have eternal life

10/31/86

The friend I never had

*And the scripture was fulfilled which saith, Abraham
believed God, and it was imputed unto him for
righteousness: and he was called the Friend of God.*

James 2:23 KJB

They say a friend is someone you can trust,
To help when struggling trials tear within;
But I never had a friend as close as Jesus;
He has forgiven and removed my every sin.

No, I never had a friend as close as Jesus,
He's a friend, a friend that always makes me glad;
He's so near and dear, and loves me as his own,
Jesus is the friend, yes He's the friend I never had.

When I was younger, I had brothers and some sisters;
We were close and shared our sorrows and our fears,
But I never had a brother close as Jesus;
All my sorrows woes and troubles Jesus hears.

No, I never had a friend as close as Jesus,
He's a friend, a friend that always makes me glad;
He's so near and dear, and loves me as his own,
Jesus is the friend, yes He's the friend I never had.

02/26/93 AEL

The hand of God

Casting all your care upon him;
for he careth for you.

1Pe 5:7

He stretched the heavens with a hand,
You see the Lord is not a man;
His majesty was always there,
He loves the weak He's always fair.

Have you wondered if the Lord did care,
If you should lose some of your hair;
Or if a button falls from your shirt,
If you fell down and got really hurt.

What does He do when you are worried,
Does He see you when you are hurried;
And when the clouds are dark around,
And all your enemies raise a sound.

Do you know what God can do,
Do you know how God loves you;
Do you know He has a plan,
Do you know you're in His hand.

Sometimes it doesn't seem that's so,
You face a struggle with a life of woe;
You wonder if He cares for you,
You let the Devil make you blue.

The Bible says we are his bride,
He's not a man, that He should lie;
We are His Jewels He loves us so,
We're in His hand, oh don't you know.

The hand of God is on His sheep,
He hears us ere' we sound a peep;
Oh little ones you should not fear,
Your God is close, He's always near.

In this final phrase I'll say,
The Hand of God will on you stay;
And if you cry to Him in prayer,
He'll answer you, you're in His care.

AEL 11/08/13

The Moon into Blood

*The sun shall be turned into darkness,
and the moon into blood, before the great
and terrible day of the LORD come.*

Joel 2:31 KJB

*And the fifth angel poured out his vial upon
the seat of the beast; and his kingdom was full of darkness;
and they gnawed their tongues for pain
And blasphemed the God of heaven because of their pains
and their sores, and repented not of their deeds.*

Rev 16:10,11 KJB

One night when all the children sleep, comes darkness
as a flood,
And God will take the yellow moon and dip it in some blood.
The tribes of earth shall mourn and cry, the least unto the best,
As an eagle mounts and spreads its wings, and scurries
from the nest;

A single prey it chases down, its claws reach out to snare,
She casts a shadow on the moon, the heavens do declare.
Her mighty wings can now be seen, against the crimson sight,
As earthly men gaze heavenly, and watch the eagle's flight

What is this sign, what is this thing, that happens in the sky?
Go sell a thing and hide your lucre, or maybe you should buy?

It won't be long before the flood, not water, I declare
But one of fire and of blood upon our nation fair.

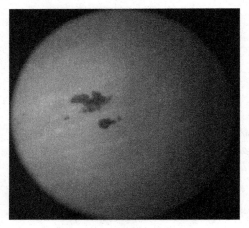

The moon of red is not alone, but a vial is also there;
And pouring out the pain and grief as much as men can bear,
Sin abounds and men relax, and play upon the green;
But the vial has an evil thing the worst t'was ever seen.

It's substance spreads among the men even as they toil;
And burns their flesh in agony, and also leaves a boil;
No children playing in the streets, they cry for milk
and bread,
and from the vial, loathsome sores cover them instead.

No man cries out to God for peace, but speaks of only war;
call out to Him, call out to God, before he shuts the door!
Watch the sky, a sign appears, a warning you will see,
For judgment comes upon the earth, and leaves no
place to flee.

5-22-09 AEL

The wicked heart

The heart is deceitful above all things,
and desperately wicked: who can know it?

Jeremiah 17:9 KJB

The heart is such a fickled thing; its wants too often change,
And in this verse, I'll try to bring our subject within range;
I'll be speaking directly to the heart; I'll bring the
matter home,
This wicked member is not fixed, it truly likes to roam.

Dear heart if I may say a word or two I know your busy now,
give to me a moment, please, as I must wipe my brow,
there, I've chased you all around the town, you never
seem to stop;
you see a thing you seem to like, and then from there you hop.

why can't you settle down and be happy with your lot,
your tangled being is always wanting what other people got;
One day you say if I only had this thing or maybe that
I'd be so happy and content; I'd keep it in my hat.

You are a wicked thing because your wants won't end,
There seem to be another thing ahead around the bend;
You love a girl. And tell her, she's all you ever need,
Then you see another girl, oh where will this all lead?

That car you got because you said I love its sleeky line,
Then you see the neighbor's truck and say it must be mine;

You had to have that T.V. set, fifty inches on the wall,
The sixty incher just came out, and you're running to the mall.

Your friends will say a word to you, that you don't really like,
So you get all offended, and tell them to take a hike;
You pout and moan and carry on, and pine away the hour,
Your like the milk left on porch, you sit and brood and sour.

Oh heart of man, what will it take to make you sit and ponder,
What spirit have you hiding there, that causes you to wander;
You will not change, you wicked heart, you'll always
be the same;
Let God come in you crippled heart; you know he
heals the lame.

The master of the universe is standing at your door,
He knocks and knocks, oh bid him, in he'll give you so
much more;
He wants to come and live with you and help you live today,
And give you life, and meaning too, all along the way.

Al Luckette 06\22\13

2Ki 5:23 And Naaman said, Be content, take two talents, And he urged him, and bound two talents of silver in two bags, with two changes of garments, and laid them upon two of his servants, and they bare them before him.

Naaman and Gehazi, servant of Elisha,

The worried heart.

Things are going pretty good, I think,
In fact, I feel I'm in the pink;
Don't get me wrong, I worry some,
Just yesterday, I did something dumb.

I worried about this pain I had,
My arm might fall off and that's bad;
I didn't know just what to do,
So I called the pastor, wouldn't you?

We shared a prayer and said good night,
I held my arm till broad daylight;
I worried that I'd lose my arm,
Or even worst I'd buy the farm.

I know to worry is not the way,
But trust in Jesus is what they say;
But I am such a worried soul,
Sometimes I could just crawl up in a hole.

Today the pain is gone from me,
The prayer we had had helped you see;
I feel so foolish to worry so,
Jesus loves me this I know.

AEL 06/30/13

The yard sale

Hurry to the open air,
Look and see what is fair;
Are you buying things today,
As you walk along the way.

See there just up the hill,
You can make it if you will;
All the buyers assembled there,
Make a bid if you dare.

Take your prize bring it home,
In the bag now your own;
What will you say to your spouse,
When you bring it to your house.

Caught up in a frenzied moment,
You bought a thing you had to own it;
I'm sure your wife will understand,
Why you bought that cast Iron bed pan.

Al Luckette 07/01/13

A Man I knew

Some time ago I knew this man,
Who only counted what was in his hand;
He worked and slaved from dawn till dark,
Always in gear, never in park.

You couldn't get one over him,
His light was on and not to dim;
he always asked for help from none,
and never stopped till he was done.

He had a wife a pretty girl,
To him she was a precious pearl;
The kids he had were his hidden jewels,
He raised them up they were nobody's fools.

But he seemed be a lonely man,
his friends were counted on one hand;
he knew he didn't find the ring,
you never heard this man to sing.

Then one day he was sighted,
To a bible study he was invited;
Oh no I can't do that right now,
It's going to snow I have to plow.

And so each time the pastor called,
In his truck and off he hauled;

He even lied and hid his face,
He would not go, or slow his pace.

But the people at the local church,
Would not be left there in the lurch;
Each day they called and off he ran,
They knew that God had called that man.

Then one day he stopped and thought,
All these years what have I fought;
I'll step aside and hear this thing,
I may even gain a ring.

He thought he 'd get a lot of strife,
But what he got was the gift of life,
His wife also yielded to the lord;
Now when you're with him you'll never be bored.

AEL.11\07\13

Today I shall be Happy

And let the peace of God rule in your hearts,
to the which also ye are called in one body;
and be ye thankful.

Colossians 3:15

Today I shall be happy,
I decree that it shall be;
I won't allow a single thing
To bother little me;
I'll look around at God's good work,
And count my blessings here,
Without a thought of anger,
'cause I know my God is near.
He opened up my eyes today,
To see the sun shine bright;
Oh how I thank my Savior,
As I'm walking in the light.
Although the snow is blowing,
And the wind is whistling too;
The heat within my spirit,
Brings sunshine out to you.
Now I can't help to smile,
My eyes are all aglow;
TODAY I SHALL BE HAPPY,
Even though I'm in the snow!

AEL

Who is that stranger?

(Lesson in humility)

*Y*ou never know who it is that comes to you. The bible speaks of Angels coming to us and we being unaware. I believe God sends help to us in different ways, for different causes, at different times. The neighbor God sends may have had a lifetime of training Just to answer your prayer. When good things keep you from better things it becomes sin.

I worked a job in a factory, and made a few friends. This one young man, Ron belonged to a CB club. The members met on occasion to talk about their experiences with their CB's. Now Ron's handle (this was the term used to describe their CB name) was crankshaft. I didn't belong to the club, But I mention this because I figured anyone with that handle had to have some experience in automobile repair. Ron's knowledge in that field was limited as I later learned, so the first lesson is you can't judge a man by his handle. Ron became a fine Christian man and an assistant Pastor, and later a Pastor.

But this story has to do with auto mechanics, which I am familiar with and have practiced most of my life. One day Ron came to me and said he was having trouble changing a starter on an old Ford car he was driving. He explained that he bought the starter and was going to change it but could not remove the old starter. He had the car jacked up in his driveway for several days and after work he would get under the car and attempt to get the old starter off. It had been raining the day he came to me and I said I would look at the car when it stopped raining. It rained heavy for two days, but on the third day it stopped. I went to his house with a few hand tools, (I like to use my own tools) I slid under the car while Ron stood in the front of the car lamenting about what a hard time he had trying to get the starter off or even loose. Meanwhile I quickly removed the starter and put the new starter in place, tightened the bolts and bolted up the hot wire. I stuck my head out and told Ron that this was going to be harder than I thought it would be and maybe he should go in the house and put a pot of coffee on. As he left I dragged the old starter out and placed it on his garage floor, Following him into the house. Ron made a pot of coffee and we sat and chatted for about half hour. I could see he became fidgety and wanted me to return to the old car, finally he said, "Okay Al don't you think we ought to get back to the starter job?" I slowly sipped the coffee then put the cup down and told him the job is done. "What? What do you mean?" he asked. "I'm done; the new starter is in the car." I replied. He was dumbfounded, and amazed that I was so quickly finished with the job that he had been working on for days.

That is the first half of the story and it was necessary to tell it so I could go on with the second half and give this lesson. The story of the Ford starter was a lesson in, "If you know your stuff the job's a breeze." Ron has many talents, a fine guitar player, much better than me, but auto repairs was not his field, he did okay but he lacked the experience, it's not a shame, or a put down, I just happened to be pressed into that field, and had a talent for handling nuts and bolts. It was a learned talent given through years of practice. I had been taking auto engines apart since I was seven. What was hard for Ron was easy for me, end of story, but hold on there is more.

About ten years later my daughter Carolyn took a job in King's Mountain, North Carolina teaching school. My wife, Fran and I took a trip down there to see her, one summer. One day after we arrived, Carolyn had to go to the town to get some stamps at the post office and mail a few letters. We left her house early and thought we would stop at the post office then visit the local town restaurant for breakfast. I was dressed in my good clothes, tan pants, and yellow shirt, I was decked out and Fran watched me closely because I always have a hard time keeping clean,

As we parked in front of the post office and started to walk to the door, I glanced to the left and noticed a car with the hood up. A young man was half buried into the engine compartment, and an older lady was setting in the passenger seat fanning herself. Three young children were running around the car playing and screaming. I instinctively started to walk towards the open hooded car. "Don't get that shirt dirty!" Fran called to me. I waved nonchalantly, without turning her way. She repeated her command, and Carolyn piped in something about going to eat and not getting greasy. I approached the car, and said, "Hi folks, having a problem?" The older lady began to lament about the heat, and the kids running around, as she kept waving a magazine in front of her face, trying to create a breeze to cool herself. She told me they were there for about two hours in the heat and she was getting sick. She told me she was praying that her son would get the car fixed so they could get out of the heat. Although it was not yet nine o'clock, the temperature was already in the high eighties. The young man pulled his head out from under the hood and said he was changing the starter on the car.

Now the car was an early Plymouth model with a slant six engine. In those cars, the starter sat on the side of the engine and was excisable from the top. I leaned into the car slightly, with my hands still in my pockets. The young man told me he was very experienced in auto repairs and began to tell me how he and a friend had once changed an engine in the friend's garage. He continued to tell me about all the tools he had, which he had there in a grip. I looked at his tools, they were a mix of old sockets and end wrenches, all mixed together in the bottom of the old grip. I began to tell him I could help him, but he interrupted me several times, telling me he was more than qualified to replace the starter. After several attempts to get close to the engine, I turned to the older woman who was still lamenting loudly about the heat and the children. I walked around to her and asked her if she was alright. She said, "I'm a praying woman." Then the old lady shouted out to God for help again. "Oh Jesus help my son to get this car fixed." I went around to the front of the car again, just as Fran and Carolyn appeared on the walk way from the post office. I could hear Fran again, "you didn't get that shirt dirty, did you? She said. I turned to her and raised my arms slightly as to say nope. Turning back to the young man I told him I hope he gets it out alright, to which he said, "No problemo, I got this!" I sort of shrugged my shoulders and walked away with Fran and Carolyn. We went to breakfast and on the way back to Carolyn's we passed the post office, and you guessed it. The old car was still there with the hood up. The young man bent over into the engine compartment, the elderly woman still waving her magazine, and the children still running around the car. Carolyn was driving, I sat in the back, I asked her to stop but I was out voted. As we drove past I watch the scene and said to myself that I should have been more forceful. Fran said something to the effect that I look for ways to get a shirt dirty.

I had to tell you the first part of this story to show you that the young man in the second part had a visitation, to help him get his car going. I was prepared to help that young man, not just prepared then, but prepared through years of struggles with life. God had prepared me with a talent. I wonder if all the learning of my trade was climaxed with that one time on the road at the post office with that lady crying out to God? But the lesson, ah yes, the lesson, had that young man knew who I was, had he humbled himself, at my service, would the outcome had been different? Of course, it would, they could have had breakfast with Fran and Carolyn and the boy with the dirty shirt. AEL

Act 3:1-3 Now Peter and John went up together into the temple at the hour of prayer, being the ninth hour. And a certain man lame from his mother's womb was carried, whom they laid daily at the gate of the temple which is called Beautiful, to ask alms of them that entered into the temple; Who seeing Peter and John about to go into the temple asked an alms.

Wise man.

I know a man who's very smart, some say he's very wise,
He's destined to greatness, his popularity on the rise;
What is his call to all this fame, why is he on the chart,
Well take at easy, less we get the horse before the cart.

All his siblings love him so, he's really on his game,
Some say you know that wisdom is synonymous
with his name;
He gives advice to anyone that ask and is sincere,
You know that if you listen, there's nothing else to fear.

Why is this man so wise, how did he learn so much,
Let's hear what he has to say, on the subject of such;
I read the bible, say my prayers, and love my God above,
I'm not a hawk, thank God, oh no, I'm just a gentle dove.

AEL.071613

You can't fool God.

In the day when God shall judge the secrets
of men by Jesus Christ according to my gospel.

Rom 2:16

Annanias and Saphira made a pledge unto the church,
They sold their land and got the dough;
and left them in the lurch,
but you can't fool God, no you can't fool God
He saw inside their hearts,
They lost their lives, in a lie that day;
From God, they had to part.

The Lord told Jonah,
preach my word to Nineveh that day;
But Jonah got into a boat and went the other way;
but you can't fool God, no you can't fool God,
If God has called you out,
You'd better do as God has said,
Then turn yourself about.

Adam and eve were told to eat
Of all the fruit but one,
The snake told eve to take a chance
Or miss out on the fun;
but you can't fool God, no you can't fool God
That couple fell from grace,

The curse of death fell onto them,
And all the human race.

Your smokescreen covers up your way,
And you think that you're alright;
You do exactly as you want,
You're okay in your sight.
but you can't fool God, no you can't fool God
He sees inside your heart,
Repent he says to you my friend,

For a new life you can start.

Chorus:
Oh you can't fool God; No you can't fool God;
He sees inside of you,
Those sins will drag you down to Hell;
Repent and be brand new!

AEL

My mom

Born to the most wonderful mother a baby could have,
mom fed me and loved me and rubbed me with salve;
mom taught me to write and read from a book,
And like most moms she really could cook.

Now mom didn't have a college degree,
But mom really knew how to take care of me;
Sometimes when I would get out of line,
Mom's little hair brush worked every time.

Mom gave me brothers and sisters a many,
Which I wouldn't swap not for a penny;
Mom let me watch them when ere she went shopping,
The five little rascals sure kept me hopping.

We traveled and traveled around this great land,
But mom never hid her head in the sand;
She faced each trial with head held high,
and oft she would tell us I'll do this or die.

She'd wash us all up each night before bed,
And though it was late and she almost dead;
She'd tell us a story, or sing us a song,
and as she would pray we followed along.

Mom taught us to live by the bible you know
She took us to church, and I'm tell'n you so;

Her spirit was meek, and often she'd cry,
And we'd bow our heads with heavy a sigh,

I remember a time we had nothing to eat,
But a bottle of ketchup, without any meat;
Mom boiled some water, out on the stoop,
And poured in the ketchup to make us some soup.

We were called the poor by all of our kin,
And having no riches they thought was a sin;
The clothing we wore, was all torn about,
But mom patched um' up, before we went out.

I love my mom, she watched over me
And all of her children she loved to a tee;
She never received an award from her peers,
But God took her home and wiped all her tears.

Mom was born on a tug, down in the city
She lived in an orphanage, oh what a pity;
She lost her mother when she was but three,
So she stayed with us close for that reason you see.

Though the trials were great, this I can say,
The Lord gave us a mom to show us the way;
Mom carried the burdens, no one could bear,
She cried for her children, I know…I was there.

Note: mother had a total of nine children, she worked in
factories, and kitchens, she washed clothes on a metal wash
board, and hung the clothes on a wire. We lived in trailers,
or tents, going from one city to the next, making due with
what we had. She taught us to read and write before we
entered kindergarten. She helped us with our home work,
so we could keep up in school She never complained, she
never gave up, she kept her kids with her through many
hard trials. She loved all her children, and prayed for our
salvation. When she could, she brought us to church. She

taught us to forgive one another, God could not have given us a better mother. I love my mother.

07\15\13 A.E.L.

Hard times.

Times were hard when I was younger,
Most the time I had a hunger;
We didn't eat three meals a day,
Mom would say, go out and play.

Times were hard when I got older
I didn't think it could get much colder;
I always seemed to have a chill,
Mom would say, here take a pill.

Times were hard when I was a teen,
Always hiding and never seen;
I didn't like to go to school,
Mom would say, hey! don't be a fool.

Times were hard for a boy like me,
Sitting under an apple tree;
The apples fell upon my head,
Mom would say it's time for bed.

Times were hard when I was bad,
It always made my father mad;
Then my hiney he would blister,
Mom would say, hey! stop it mister.

Ya, times were hard, I have to say,
But it was better than today;

See, I had mom to guide me then,
And ere I went she would defend,

The Lord was watching over me,
He sent his angel can't you see,
God put me in a training place
Those hard times helped me run the race.

Al Luckette 04/03/2000

Dingle Hole Road

Dingle Hole Road was an old dirt road, up in New York State;
We were just poor folks there, with not much on the plate.
Had some chickens in the yard, eggs we had a few;
Chopped off their heads, when things got tight, this story's really true.

Had no 'letric from the pole, a lamp was all we had;
Did my homework in the dark, boy my grades were bad.
Dug a hole in the back yard, a new well for the land;
The walls caved in, I nearly died, from digging in the sand.

Got our water from the well, out front with rope and pail;
Washed in a tub, upon the stove, every Saturday without fail.
Dingle Hole Road was an old dirt road, the school a mile away;
It had one room, for one through nine, I went most every day.

An old shed sat behind the house, of course without a heater,
When I looked in to my surprise, we had an old two seater.
My brother Paul would chase the rabbits, he'd catch them in his hand;
He chased them high, he chased them low, on twenty three acres of land.

A bald necked rooster in the yard, thought that he was king;
He picked a fight with a bantam knight, and got knocked
out 'o the ring.
We burned some cars out in the yard, so we could junk
the metal;
We drained the oil in a pan, t'was ma's old cooking kettle.

Dingle Hole Road was an old dirt road, I loved to walk
it's trail;
R.F.D. was our address, when ere we got some mail.
Family came to visit us, they brought some food one day,;
They left it on the table there, and quickly went away.

Those toilet seats in winter time, on dingle hole were cold;
When I sat down, it weren't for long, and now the story's told.

Al Luckette 12/05/08